I0814221

BETTER *at* HOME

COLU HENRY

Photography by

SILVER UND SECK

Recipes for Big Nights In

ABRAMS, NEW YORK

To the women in my life who mothered me when I most needed to be mothered.

&

For the love of all dogs, past and present.

Chapter 1
SNACKY BITS AND SIPS

Chapter 2
VEG

Chapter 3
IN BOWLS

Chapter 4
PASTA POTS AND PIZZA PIES

Introduction

I love going out for dinner. There is nothing better than sidling up to a bar, ordering an ice-cold martini, crab cocktail, and a side of fries and having someone make it all for you. The luxury of having a big, beautiful bowl of silky pasta placed down in front of you followed by an espresso and an amaro (with one cube) for dessert will never be lost on me. I still make my dad take me to lunch at any steakhouse that will have me, because being in a low-lit, old-school environment, preferably in midtown, will always give me a thrill. Ditto on fancy hotel bars.

The energy of good restaurants is palpable and sexy, and I have spent countless hours both front and back of house. Throughout college in Boston, I worked as a barista, a cocktail waitress, and a bartender. And again, as a brasserie bartender my first four years in New York City, while I also was a cabaret singer—not at the brasserie . . . Between pouring middle-aged men too much scotch and performing in Times Square and Arlene's Grocery on the Lower East Side, I saw a lot. So perhaps it is no surprise that I graduated from working in restaurants, to working for them.

In my midtwenties, in the early aughts, after a few years working in fashion public relations, I was once again drawn back to hospitality and took a food writing class, which led me to a job in restaurant and chef PR. For someone whose quest was to learn everything she could about food and not have to work night shifts, it was a pretty good place to start.

I lived paycheck to paycheck, but what a time to be alive. To give you a sense, at a birthday party someone mistook my husband, Chad, for Rocco DiSpirito and chaos nearly ensued. This was just when it became status quo to have agency representation for big openings and I was lucky enough to work with some of the very best chefs and restaurateurs. Stephen Starr, Marcus Samuelsson, and Scott Conant were among them. You can imagine, I was very popular with my friends for snagging hard-to-get reservations at places like Alto, Buddakan, and Morimoto in their heyday.

The job entailed many things, including legitimately tasting everything on the menu, sometimes multiple times, and writing pages of tasting notes to share as feedback. In addition, I was also in charge of cleaning up and editing chefs' recipes to make them legible for publications as well as to produce any photo shoot or TV segment that needed producing. I learned so much and had a blast doing it. In fact, all of these skills are needed when writing a cookbook, which I didn't see coming at the time, but makes absolutely perfect sense to me now.

There were also some very late nights wining and dining journalists, hanging out with chefs, attending events, and a lot of other mischief not suitable to print, but that's what being in your twenties in New York City is about.

After a brief stint in Portland, Oregon, working in wine, I landed back in New York City at *Bon Appétit*. You can't take this girl off the East Coast for long… At Condé Nast, I learned the publishing side of the business and straddled both the editorial and business side, where I helped to head up PR and special projects. Like most jobs, it was great, until it wasn't. But I did learn an incredible amount about the storytelling process and on my way out I got my first book deal.

These days, I split my time between Hudson, New York, and the north shore of Nova Scotia where Chad and I are restoring an 1866 farmhouse by the sea. My life is beautiful and full and busy, but it also doesn't look the same way it once did. The truth is, I don't want to be out every night of the week anymore. I much prefer the comfort of my own home (or someone else's) to cook or be cooked for. I want to be in charge of the guest list, the menu, the music, and the overall vibe. This also changes based on where we are. In Hudson, we wander back and forth between friends' homes. Some nights we head next door to Kelly's for a quick curry or a pasta, to our friend Annabel's for roast chicken or steak au poivre on toast. A Friday night happy hour at our septuagenarian friends Paula and Phil's complete with her chopped liver and his martinis are a treat, and a Saturday afternoon spent with our friends Harry and Sophie pressing their delicious, dry cider is almost wholesome. The holidays are spent with our chosen family, Dan and Helen, where we camp out at their house for days, eating, cooking, and imbibing, each of us taking turns in front of the stove. There is always a Christmas Lasagna, and Boxing Day wouldn't be complete without bacon sarnies . . . Our friends Emma and Dom have claimed Guy Fawkes night as their annual UK holiday, fit with honey and mustard sausages served in bread, pork pies, and a big bonfire. And, sitting in front of a roaring fireplace with a table full of snacks at our friend Hélène and John's is a perfect evening. Dogs are of course encouraged and included at every occasion. There are many dinner parties, and with the agriculture bounty of the Hudson Valley and access to any ingredient, it's easy.

In Nova Scotia, I cook a bit differently, not dramatically so, but more simply than I do in Hudson. I pack up most of my pantry before we make the eleven-hour drive east to the Maritimes for summer. For example, Diamond Crystal kosher salt is hard to come by, so I bring my own. Grated Locatelli pecorino, too. We are in a very rural area, and while I can go up the road for meat at a local farm, or to the lobster pound, the closest grocery store is a thirty-minute drive away. Produce is still sourced from a nearby farm, but instead of having the option of say ten varietals of tomatoes and peppers, there are more likely around two. I will say the new potatoes grown in the thick, red, muddy soil are outstanding and when boiled and tossed with too much salted butter, you'd be hard pressed to want anything but! My cooking is more straightforward, but no less delicious. This house, too, is almost always filled with visiting friends. We have a wood-fired pizza oven, which we use often. And luckily, our dear pals Andy and Rachel bought a house up the road and Sunday is our pizza date night for the months of July and August. I find it inspiring to cook within constraints. And, side note, the joy of having an apple tree in the backyard that I can pick fruit from to make a quick cake is incredibly fulfilling.

My point is, I suppose, is that it's not just me. Our group, of course, loves a city trip, a pub crawl, and getting dressed up to dine out on occasion, but what's really filling our collective cups is being together where and whenever we want on our own terms. *Better at Home* embraces all of that and the in between. I'm so grateful you're here.

A morning in Peggy's Cove.

Shopping Suggestions

This is not a proper pantry section. It's more suggestions of what to keep on hand. I only use Diamond Crystal kosher salt for cooking. First and foremost, if I call out a specific amount and you're not using this brand and are using Morton's or another kind, you generally want to halve the amount or it will be too salty.

These are spices, nuts, seeds, fridge things, and more that I call on frequently throughout the book. Given I've asked you to purchase them, I wanted you to get multiple uses out of ingredients rather than having random "called for items" that will linger in your pantry and fridge for months. I also consider the fridge part of my pantry, it's just at a cooler temperature (aka the "cold pantry"), and when all are smartly stocked it's incredibly helpful to pull together flavorful and impressive dishes. Think citrus, condiments, pickles, and pastes. I'm hopeful you'll find this helpful.

IN THE SPICE DRAWER:

Black peppercorns
Cumin: both seeds and ground
Diamond Crystal kosher salt
Dried mint
Fennel seeds
Red pepper flakes
Sesame seeds

PICKLES, PASTES, PRESERVES:

Calabrian chili paste or pickles
Castelvetrano olives
Cento hoagie spread
Chili crisp
Cornichons
Harissa paste
Miso
'Nduja
Preserved lemon paste or whole lemons
Tahini
Tomato paste

IN THE "PANTRY PANTRY":

Anchovies
Better than Bouillon
Dates
Dried and/or canned beans
Extra virgin olive oil
Fried shallots
Garlic
Good-quality vinegars: red wine, white wine, cider, and sherry
Grapeseed or other neutral oil
Honey
Light brown sugar
Maille Dijon mustard
Nuts: pistachios, walnuts, almonds, and hazelnuts
Panko bread crumbs
Pasta: both long and short shapes
Rice wine
Soy sauce
Toasted sesame oil
Tomato passata or canned tomatoes

IN THE "COLD PANTRY":

Assorted citrus
Butter
Eggs
Feta cheese
Fresh herbs: such as Italian parsley, cilantro, green onions, and mint
Fresh mozzarella
Half-and-half or heavy cream
Onions and shallots
Pancetta or bacon
Pecorino or Parmesan cheese
Sour cream

RUMMO
RUMMO
PENNE RIGATE N°66
GLUTEN FREE
FARRO
CAMPANINI
HEINZ
BEANS
RUMMO
MATHESON
FOOD
COMPANY
ORIGINAL
ORIGINALE
MUTTI
MUTTI
MUTTI
Cherry
TOMATO
PASTE
DIAMOND
CRYSTAL
Wonderful
Robin Hood
TOUT USAGE
RANCHO GORDO
RANCHO GORDO
JACOBSEN
SALT CO.
PURE ITALIAN
FINE SEA SALT
KIKKOMAN

SNACKY BITS *AND* SIPS

Fizzy Negroni Pompelmo

MAKES
1 cocktail

TIME
5 minutes

INGREDIENTS
- 2 ounces (60 ml) gin
- 2 ounces (60 ml) sweet vermouth
- 2 ounces (60 ml) Campari
- 1 ounce (30 ml) grapefruit juice
- Splash of prosecco or other sparkling white wine
- Grapefruit twist, for garnish

I love Negronis—who doesn't? Personally, when I start making this classic Italian cocktail, it signals that the weather has turned brisk and we're now relegated to drinking indoors for the next few months. They are a perfect way to start off the night. In this version I've added some grapefruit juice for a bit of punch and some bubbles for festivity.

METHOD

In an ice-filled cocktail shaker, combine the gin, vermouth, Campari, and grapefruit juice and stir together briskly until very cold. Strain into a rocks glass filled with ice. Top with the prosecco and garnish with a grapefruit twist.

Spicy *and* Jammy Agrodolce Peppers *with* Fried Salumi

SERVES
4

TIME
30 minutes

INGREDIENTS

¼ cup (60 ml) good-quality balsamic vinegar

1 tablespoon light brown sugar

2 tablespoons extra-virgin olive oil, plus more as needed

3 ounces (85 g) hard dried salumi, such as soppressata or finocchiona, cut into ¼-inch (6 mm) dice

6 cloves garlic, smashed and peeled

1 teaspoon red pepper flakes (half if you don't like heat)

1 pound (455 g) small sweet peppers, preferably a mixture of red, yellow, and orange

Kosher salt and freshly ground black pepper

2 tablespoons roughly chopped fresh Italian parsley, for serving

Flaky salt, for serving

These peppers work equally well for happy hour as they do as a starter or side. They are pleasantly piquant and when tossed in a glaze of balsamic vinegar and brown sugar, everything is nicely balanced. Fried salumi adds a hit of saltiness and a nice textural element, but feel free to leave it out should you want the dish to be vegetarian.

METHOD

In a small bowl, whisk together the balsamic vinegar and brown sugar until it dissolves and set aside.

Line a plate with paper towels and have near the stove. In a heavy-bottomed 12-inch (30 cm) skillet, heat the olive oil over medium heat until it shimmers. Add the salumi and cook, stirring occasionally until crispy, 2 to 3 minutes. With a slotted spoon, transfer to the paper towels.

Reduce the heat to medium-low and add the garlic and pepper flakes. Cook, stirring occasionally, until the garlic starts to turn golden, a few minutes more. Transfer to the plate with the salumi.

Turn the heat back up to medium, add the peppers and season with salt and black pepper, adding a bit more oil if the pan is dry. Cook, stirring often, until they start turning brown and golden in spots, pressing them with the back of a spoon if needed to help them fully soften, 10 to 15 minutes.

Return the salumi and garlic to the pan. Pour in the vinegar and sugar mixture, it may bubble slightly, that's OK, and stir until everything is coated and glossy with the sauce. Transfer to a bowl or platter and scatter with parsley. Season with a few pinches of flaky salt.

Italian Shrimp Toast

SERVES
4 to 6

TIME
20 minutes

INGREDIENTS

6 ounces (170 g) shrimp, preferably wild-caught, peeled and deveined
1½ ounces (40 g) 'nduja
1 small shallot, halved
2 cloves garlic, roughly chopped
1 rosemary sprig, leaves picked and roughly chopped
1 teaspoon fennel seeds
1 (2-inch/5 cm) strip lemon zest
½ teaspoon red pepper flakes
½ teaspoon kosher salt
1 teaspoon extra-virgin olive oil, plus more for shallow-frying
6 slices white sandwich bread, such as Pepperidge Farm
5 tablespoons (50 g) toasted sesame seeds
Flaky salt, for serving
1 lemon, for serving
1 tablespoon finely chopped chives

Chad and I will often drive from Hudson to Albany for good Chinese food, because I love it so much. This recipe is inspired by the Cantonese dim sum dish from Hong Kong. In lieu of Asian flavors, I take this one in the Italian direction, making a paste of shrimp, 'nduja (a spicy spreadable sausage from Calabria), fennel seeds, lemon zest, and some other traditional aromatics. These toasts are incredibly delicious and rich and work well for a casual (or not) cocktail hour with something bright, white, and crisp poured alongside.

METHOD

In a food processor, pulse together the shrimp, 'nduja, shallot, garlic, rosemary, fennel seeds, lemon zest, pepper flakes, salt, and olive oil. Scrape into a bowl.

With a small offset spatula or spoon, smear the shrimp paste "wall to wall" on one side of each slice of bread.

Pour the sesame seeds into a shallow bowl or plate. Dip the bread shrimp side down into the sesame seeds, pressing the bread to make sure they evenly adhere to the shrimp mixture.

In a deep skillet, pour in enough olive oil to come halfway up the side of the bread. Heat over medium-high heat. Sprinkle a bit of salt into the oil to make sure it is hot enough; if it sizzles you're ready to shallow-fry.

Line a baking sheet with paper towels and have near the stove. Working in batches to not overcrowd the pan, add the bread shrimp side down and cook until golden, 1 to 2 minutes. Flip and cook 1 more minute more.

Place the toast on the paper towels, season with flaky salt, and allow to cool for a minute or so.

Plate on a platter or large dish and give them a good squeeze of lemon. Scatter with chives. Pass the toasts with cocktail napkins and more lemon wedges.

A Note: Should you want to get ahead of things, you can make and freeze the paste a few days beforehand. Allow to come to room temperature before spreading.

Fried Sausage-Stuffed Olives

MAKES
14 stuffed olives

TIME
40 minutes

INGREDIENTS

- 4 ounces (115 g) pitted Castelvetrano olives (about 14)
- 12 ounces (340 g) sweet Italian sausages (about 3 links), casings removed
- 2 ounces (55 g) grated pecorino (I like Locatelli), plus more for serving
- ⅛ teaspoon freshly grated nutmeg
- ¼ to ½ teaspoon red pepper flakes (optional)
- Freshly ground black pepper
- ¾ cup (95 g) all-purpose flour
- 2 large eggs, whisked
- 1¼ cups (100 g) panko bread crumbs
- 4 cups (960 ml) peanut oil, for shallow-frying

This recipe is inspired by my lovely friend Steph who visited me from Naples, Italy, over the holidays a few years back. She came to Hudson to teach me how to make tortellini in brodo from scratch (see my new take on page 96) and we had lots of leftover filling to put to use. She suggested stuffing buttery Castelvetrano olives with our leftovers and then dredging them in bread crumbs before shallow-frying until crispy. Who am I to disagree? They were a delicious, salty, crunchy, and perfect aperitivo snack. I simplified the recipe by using Italian sausage, which already has so much flavor. You'll want to serve these hot and preferably paired with a glass of something bubbly. Fried and fizzy are a perfect match.

METHOD

With a paring knife, gently slice lengthwise through one side of the olive, repeat with remaining olives. Set aside.

In a medium bowl, combine the sausage, pecorino, a few gratings of nutmeg, pepper flakes (if using), and a few turns of black pepper. Using your hands or a spoon, stir until everything is well combined.

Take a small pinch of the filling and stuff inside each of the olives. Press some of the remaining filling around the outside of each olive, rolling to completely cover the olive with the sausage mixtures and form a small, meatball-looking shape.

Set up a dredging station in three shallow bowls: Place the flour in one, the eggs in a second, and the panko in the third. Working in batches, roll the olives in flour, shaking off any excess, then dip into the eggs, and then dredge in the panko.

Line a plate with paper towels and have near the stove. In a large soup pot or Dutch oven, heat the oil over medium heat until a deep-fry thermometer reads 350°F (177°C).

Working in batches, carefully fry until the olives turn golden brown and crispy, 3 to 4 minutes per batch. Remove from the oil with a spider strainer and place on the paper towels to drain.

Transfer to a platter, sprinkle with some more pecorino, and serve.

Crab Mayonnaise-y *with* Toast

SERVES
4 to 6

TIME
20 minutes

INGREDIENTS

- 8 ounces (225 g) picked crab meat, preferably Dungeness
- ½ cup (120 ml) Immersion Blender Aioli (page 229), made with Meyer lemon juice
- 4 to 6 slices sourdough bread or white sandwich bread, toasted
- Lemon wedges and flaky salt, for serving
- Roughly chopped tender herbs (optional), such as Italian parsley, chives, or tarragon

My dearest friend, Helen, and I love crab. Out of all the shellfish, I can confidently say it's our favorite. Whilst sitting at the bar sipping martinis at Keens Steakhouse in New York City, the crab cocktail (and French fries) is our regular order, and in fact anywhere else that crab is available and we are together we order it then, too. Helen and I also love the holidays. And in celebration of our chosen family, each year for Christmas Eve, I order Dungeness crab from Pike Place Market in Seattle to have for our Feast of the Seven Fishes celebration. In my opinion, it is sweet and superior. I make aioli and swap regular lemons for the Meyer variety as they are finally in season, toast thick slices of sourdough bread, and put out piles of crab for everyone to make their own crab toast. Of course, you could mix the crab and aioli together for a more formal "dish," but to me the unfussiness of it all makes it even more elegant, especially when eaten with good friends.

METHOD

Arrange the crab and aioli in separate, thoughtful bowls with a spoon and a knife. Arrange the bread on a plate or board.

Encourage friends to make their own toast. I like to put the crab on top of a piece of toast with ample amounts of aioli swooped on top. Helen reverses this method and there is no right or wrong way. There is just your way. Top each piece with a squeeze of lemon, a pinch of flaky salt, and some herbs, should you like.

Scallop Crudo *with* Blood Orange *and* Mint

SERVES
4

TIME
20 minutes

INGREDIENTS

- Grated zest and juice of 1 blood orange
- 6 to 8 large scallops (preferably wild-caught), very thinly sliced horizontally with a very sharp knife
- 1 red serrano chile, sliced into thin rings
- Good-quality olive oil, for drizzling (about 1½ tablespoons)
- 1 tablespoon finely chopped fresh mint
- 1 tablespoon minced fresh chives
- Flaky salt, for finishing

People can be intimidated by preparing and serving raw fish at home, but as long as you're buying the freshest available, you've got nothing to worry about. The citrus cures the shellfish, so I suppose technically it's not *raw* raw, but you get the picture. Crudo, specifically made with scallops, is one of my favorite dishes; and as a special treat, I made this for my birthday dinner a few years back. I also bought myself a white truffle—what can I say, I was feeling extravagant! Blood oranges come into season early winter, so if you can find one to use, please do. They offer a lovely, floral note and their vibrant color can't be beat. If not, feel free to use a lemon, lime, or grapefruit or a combination of all three.

METHOD

In a bowl, stir together the blood orange zest and juice.

Evenly distribute the scallops among four small plates and top each with some of the serrano chile. Spoon some of the blood orange zest/juice mixture over each serving. Drizzle with a generous teaspoon or so of the olive oil. Scatter each plate with some of the mint and the chives and finish with a good pinch of flaky salt.

A Note: This dish would be a lovely start to any meal, but particularly nice if you're celebrating Feast of the Seven Fishes. It's not heavy, leaving you room for six more fishes!

A Garden Party

MAKES
1 cocktail

TIME
5 minutes

INGREDIENTS

3 ounces (90 ml) Tito's vodka or other vodka of your choice

1 ounce (30 ml) dry vermouth

A fancy toothpick with a cornichon, cocktail onion, and Castelvetrano olive, for garnish

The truth is I drink martinis year-round, but around the holidays they fall into more of a regular rotation. Over the years, I've gone from being a lemon twist gal to preferring olives and then, out of nowhere, I was suddenly a diehard Gibson girl. I've evolved yet again and now take my drink with a cornichon, a perfectly puckery pickled onion (they are in the same jar!), and a buttery olive all in the same glass and named it A Garden Party. If you like Cheddar cheese and onion sandwiches and oysters and sausages for dinner, I think you'll like this, too.

METHOD

Fill a martini glass or other cocktail glass of your choosing with ice water.

In an ice-filled cocktail shaker, combine the vodka and vermouth and shake until very chilled and you can barely hold the shaker. Discard the ice water and strain the mixture into the chilled glass. Garnish with the cornichon- onion-and-olive toothpick.

Smashed Potatoes *with* Sour Cream *and* Caviar

SERVES
4 to 6

TIME
1 hour 20 minutes

INGREDIENTS
2 pounds (910 g) new or small waxy potatoes
½ cup (67 g) kosher salt, plus more for seasoning
½ cup (120 ml) extra-virgin olive oil
Freshly ground black pepper
2 to 3 ounces (55 to 85 g) Ossetra caviar or trout roe
1½ cups (360 ml) sour cream
2 tablespoons finely chopped fresh chives

I made our friends Emma and Dom smashed potatoes for a dinner in our Hudson backyard on a late night in June. Months later she texted me for the recipe, which I happily shared, but it wasn't until I saw her in person that she told me she not only made the potatoes for Christmas Day, but she served them with sour cream and caviar. Genius! Clearly this is a celebratory dish as caviar ain't cheap, but it's so worth it, especially if you're hosting someone or something festive. Serve with lots of champagne.

METHOD

Preheat the oven to 400°F (200°C).

In a large soup pot, combine the potatoes, salt, and water to cover by 1 to 2 inches and bring to a boil. Cook, until you can pierce them easily with a fork, about 15 minutes. Drain.

Spray a large sheet pan with cooking spray. Arrange the potatoes on the pan and with the bottom of a mug or a measuring cup, smash each of the potatoes until they just fall apart. Drizzle with the olive oil and season well with salt and pepper.

Roast, until they are golden and crispy, 30 to 35 minutes.

Just before serving, lay out your sour cream, caviar, and chives.

Remove the potatoes from the oven and place on a plate or large platter. Serve immediately alongside the sour cream and caviar and encourage guests to make their own and top with chives.

The Ventura: An Amaro Spritz

MAKES
1 cocktail

TIME
5 minutes

INGREDIENTS

- 2 ounces (60 ml) amaro, such as Cynar, Faccia Bruto, or Averna
- 4 ounces (120 ml) club soda
- Fresh lemon juice
- Strip of lemon peel, for garnish

One early January, our friends Michael and Caroline Ventura came for a long-overdue Hudson visit. At our favorite local restaurant, Rivertown Tavern, Michael ordered an amaro and soda before dinner. I tasted it and didn't know why I had never done so before. I love amaro! Why NOT top it with soda?! This drink is the perfect way to start off an aperitivo hour, and given they are incredibly delicious it also makes it hard to stop drinking them . . . The truth is it's equally good at the end of an evening. I've named this cocktail after Michael and it's now The Ventura and it remains in constant rotation.

METHOD

Fill a large wine glass with ice. Add the amaro, top with the club soda, and a squeeze of lemon juice. Give it a good, quick stir and garnish with the lemon peel.

A Note: While visiting Michael at his home on Shelter Island, he served this drink to me alongside a snack he called Egg Bread. As soon as I smelled it coming from the kitchen, I knew it was a very similar version of the same batter that I use to fry eggplant, chicken, and stuffed squash blossoms. We are very alike in our cooking styles. To make it yourself, thinly slice a few pieces of bread, make the egg batter from page 41, and shallow-fry the bread in a bit of olive oil until golden. Top with confited cherry tomatoes, mozzarella, and anchovies or simply on its own—it's perfect as is.

Spicy Shrimp Butter

SERVES
6 to 8

TIME
20 minutes

INGREDIENTS

Kosher salt
½ pound (225 g) wild-caught shrimp, peeled and deveined
1 medium shallot, roughly chopped
2 oil-packed anchovy fillets
¼ cup (8 g) loosely packed fresh Italian parsley, both leaves and tender stems
8 tablespoons (115 g/1 stick) unsalted butter, at room temperature
1 teaspoon grated Meyer lemon or regular lemon zest
2 tablespoons Meyer lemon or regular lemon juice, plus more to taste
1 teaspoon Calabrian chili paste
Triscuits and crudités, for serving.

This retro-inspired snacking butter will be a hit at any cocktail party. It's best served right away but can be made a day in advance; just be sure to bring it to room temperature before serving to maximize its spreadability. I love serving this dip with Triscuits, but any cracker will suit. Leftovers can be stirred into pasta.

METHOD

Set up a large bowl of ice and water and have near the stove. Bring a large pot of salted water to a boil. Reduce the heat to a simmer and add the shrimp. Cook until the shrimp are completely pink and firm to the touch, 2 to 3 minutes. Transfer to the ice bath and let sit until cool enough to handle and then pat them dry.

Transfer the shrimp to a food processor along with the shallot, anchovies, and parsley and pulse together until they form a paste.

In a large bowl, beat the butter with a wooden spoon or spatula until smooth. Transfer the shrimp paste to the bowl of butter, along with the lemon zest, lemon juice, Calabrian chili paste, and a good pinch of salt. Stir together until everything is well combined. Taste and adjust with more lemon juice and salt if needed.

Transfer to a shallow bowl and serve immediately with crackers and crudité.

Hélène's Roasted Olive Dip *with* Za'atar *and* Sumac

SERVES
4 to 6

TIME
20 minutes

INGREDIENTS

- 1 ½ cups (360 ml) plain Icelandic Provisions skyr (you can also use plain Greek yogurt or labneh)
- 1 clove garlic, grated
- 1 teaspoon kosher salt, plus more to taste
- 1 cup (150 g) pitted olives, any kind or a mixture, so long as they're pitted (she likes Castelvetrano, as do I!)
- 1 to 2 tablespoons crushed Calabrian chilis and their oil (optional), to taste
- 1 heaping tablespoon Les Herbes Salées du Bas-du-Fleuve (see Note)
- 3 thinly sliced lemon rounds (optional)
- 1 tablespoon extra-virgin olive oil, plus more for serving
- 1 tablespoon ground sumac
- 1 tablespoon za'atar
- 3 tablespoons torn, mixed fresh herbs, such as mint, dill, and parsley (or just one, whatever you have on hand)
- Crusty sourdough or pita chips, for serving

My dear friend Hélène is the consummate hostess. Everything she does is thoughtful and picture perfect; she also has a heart of gold. We've spent many weekend nights at her and her husband John's beautiful home snacking on her beautiful spreads and sipping wine in front of their enormous fireplace. Hélène makes different versions of this dip, which I always request, and they are all wonderful, but this one is my favorite. Les Herbes Salées du Bas-du-Fleuve, salted preserved herbs that are a tradition from Québec, are called for as she hails from Montreal. If you happen to stumble across them, they are worthy of picking up. That said, this dip is equally splendid utilizing a combination of fresh and dried herbs. It's also easy on the eyes, just like her.

METHOD

Preheat the oven to 425°F (220°C).

Meanwhile, in a medium bowl, mix together the skyr, garlic, and salt. Taste and season with more salt as needed. Cover and refrigerate until ready to assemble.

On a lined sheet pan, mix together the olives, Calabrian chili (if using), herbes salées, lemon rounds (if using), and the olive oil to coat everything. Transfer to the oven.

Roast until the olives are tender and slightly shriveled, 20 to 25 minutes. If they need more time, stir the mix and roast another 5 minutes. Remove from the oven and discard the lemon if used.

Grab your skyr from the fridge and transfer it to a small to medium shallow serving bowl. Create a ring around the edge with your spoon leaving a ¼-inch (6 mm) border and a small well in the center.

Carefully spoon the roasted olive mixture onto the skyr, filling the bowl up to the ring well. Make sure you add all the juices from the roasted mixture. Sprinkle evenly with the sumac, then the za'atar. Top with the fresh herbs and a drizzle of olive oil.

Serve with crusty sourdough or pita chips.

A Note: To substitute for the herbes salées, use leaves from 3 thyme sprigs, 1 teaspoon dried oregano, 1 teaspoon dried parsley, and a generous pinch of kosher salt.

Stuffed *and* Egg-Battered Squash Blossoms

SERVES
2 or 3 and is easily doubled

TIME
30 minutes

INGREDIENTS

for the blossoms and filling:

- 1 ounce (28 g) squash blossoms (about 6)
- 5 ounces (140 g) whole-milk ricotta cheese
- 2 tablespoons finely chopped fresh mint
- ½ teaspoon grated lemon zest
- 3 tablespoons grated pecorino cheese
- Kosher salt and freshly ground black pepper

for the batter and frying:

- 2 large eggs
- 2 tablespoons finely chopped fresh Italian parsley
- 2 tablespoons finely chopped fresh chives
- ¼ cup (25 g) grated pecorino cheese
- Kosher salt and freshly ground black pepper
- About ½ cup (120 ml) extra-virgin olive oil, for shallow-frying
- Flaky salt, for serving

The batter for these squash blossoms is one that I return to frequently. It's how I fry my eggplant for eggplant Parmesan, how I fry chicken cutlets, and how my friend Michael makes his Egg Bread (see Note, page 34). It's very good. It also makes this version of stuffed squash blossoms much more delicate than how they are traditionally prepared, which is heavily breaded. Their season is so fleeting, it's nice to let them have their moment, and this delicate batter allows them to. I add some mint and lemon zest to the creamy filling; basil or parsley would also be nice. You will likely have a tablespoon or so of leftover filling. This is a perfect chef's treat or if you happen to have another blossom, I suppose you could fill it.

METHOD

Remove the stamen from each of the squash blossoms and discard. Set aside the squash blossoms while you make the filling.

Make the filling: In a medium bowl, combine the ricotta, mint, lemon zest, and pecorino. Season with salt and a few grinds of the black pepper. Stir together to combine, taste, and adjust seasonings accordingly with salt.

Transfer the mixture to a zip-top plastic bag and gather the filling on the bottom on one side and snip the corner with kitchen shears. Pipe some of the ricotta filling into each of the blossoms leaving a bit of room at the top to twist closed. Set aside while you make the batter.

Make the batter: In a bowl, whisk together the eggs, parsley, chives, pecorino, a good pinch of salt, and a few grinds of black pepper.

Fry the blossoms: Line a plate with paper towels and have near the stove. In a large skillet, heat the oil over medium heat. Add a few drops of batter to test when the oil is hot enough to fry. If it bubbles up, you're ready.

One by one, gently coat the stuffed blossoms in the batter. Add to the oil without crowding the pan and cook until golden, about 2 minutes per side. Transfer to the paper towels to drain and season with a few pinches of flaky salt.

Serve right away.

A Lobster Dip Welcome

SERVES
4 to 8, depending on your ramekin journey

TIME
25 minutes

INGREDIENTS

Softened butter, for the ramekin(s)
2 tablespoons (30 g) unsalted butter
1 shallot, minced
Kosher salt
1 block (8 ounces/225 g) cream cheese, at room temperature
8 ounces (225 g) lobster meat
2 ounces (55 g) shredded mozzarella cheese
1 tablespoon México Lindo or other hot sauce of your choosing
1 teaspoon grated lemon zest
2 teaspoons fresh lemon juice
Freshly ground black pepper

for serving:
Sliced vegetables, such as cucumber, fennel, endive, celery, and radishes
Crackers

More often than not, when our friends arrive at The Windy Poplars for their Nova Scotia vacation, it's too late for lunch, but too early for dinner. This means it's a "snacks for supper" affair (see Snacking Peppers on page 52), which I love to assemble. Everyone is excited to be reunited and there is always much chatter and catching up to do. I prep this dip ahead so when they do arrive, all I need to do is heat up the oven, slice up some vegetables, pull some cheese and cured meats, and open some wine. I prefer to make this dip and divide it into two 4-ounce (120 ml) ramekins, because that means we'll have some to warm up the next evening after a long beach day. But, should you want a larger serving to feed more people, use a single 8-ounce (240 ml) ramekin instead.

METHOD

Preheat the oven to 375°F (190°C). Butter an 8-ounce (240 ml) ramekin or two 4-ounce (120 ml) ramekins.

In a medium skillet, melt the 2 tablespoons butter over medium heat. Add the shallot and cook until softened, about 3 minutes. Season with salt and remove from the heat.

In a large bowl, combine the shallots, cream cheese, lobster meat, mozzarella, hot sauce, lemon zest, and lemon juice. Stir well to combine. Taste and season with salt and black pepper to taste. With a spoon or spatula, add the lobster mixture to the ramekin(s). I like to pile it high. Set on a baking sheet.

Bake until everything is warmed through and the cheese has melted, 15 to 20 minutes. Turn the broiler to high and cook for a minute or two until golden in spots.

Serve warm.

The Tides

In the summer I live by the tides. It's hard to do otherwise and I am happier for it. It gives me some sense of structure in a lackadaisical season with little agency. I am not complaining. Plans are made, schedules coordinated, and picnics are collaborated on by these tide times. There are conversations about what we'd prefer—to walk the flats and see Sugo the dog sprint across the sand at low tide while the water slowly and then suddenly all at once comes up in pools around us. Or is a higher tide swim preferred? This is usually followed by a barbecue with cold beers and wine in the backyard among the apple trees. Both are lovely and different and some days we are lucky enough to do both.

Should we go at low tide, I pack simple sandwiches of cheese and onion and cucumber on pedestrian, but perfect, sandwich bread. It's a sandwich reminiscent of my childhood summers on the Cape. As a young girl, my mother stuffed pitas with Havarti cheese, sprouts, and cucumber and slathered them with mayonnaise, to eat sitting at the base of the dunes of Cahoon Hollow beach in Wellfleet. Eating one now while on the red sand beach of the north shore in Nova Scotia takes me back to a time of innocence and happiness when my family was one unit and I was blissfully unaware of anything otherwise. It's a brief, nostalgic respite.

When we go at high tide, it is usually a quick dip. There is no beach to sit on, so logically we'll work our way back to the house picking wild raspberries that grow on the side of the road as a reward snack for our absolutely *tremendous* effort. Depending on the time of day, Chad will put coals on to grill sausages, or clams (page 174), or start a fire for the pizza oven.

It stays light outside past 9 p.m. in high summer and late lunches and dinners are eaten around a modest, weathered wood table on the back deck. It is all very convivial and casual. As the sun dips below the horizon, the sky turns beautiful shades of deep corals and salmon. It simultaneously signifies that it's time to quickly move festivities inside. The mosquitoes are also about to dine out and they always mean business. I'll check the tide times once again before it's lights out and start plotting the next day's adventures. I very much love spending my summers by the sea.

A Perfect Beach Sandwich

SERVES
2

TIME
5 minutes

INGREDIENTS

4 slices of your favorite squishy white sandwich bread

Plenty of Hellmann's mayonnaise

4 thin slices of Havarti cheese

2 Persian (mini) cucumber, thinly sliced on the bias

Thinly sliced white onion

Kosher salt and freshly ground black pepper

Beach sandwiches are subjective. This is how I like mine. Simple and best eaten with a good friend overlooking the water. Swap out any cheese you choose. Serve with salt and vinegar potato chips and a cold beer on a beach blanket.

METHOD

Slather 2 slices of the bread with as much mayonnaise as you deem appropriate, I like a fair amount. On the other slices, add the cheese, cucumbers (set on an angle to fit the shape of the bread), and top with the onion. Season liberally with salt and pepper. Top the vegetable and cheese side with the one slathered with mayo and press down firmly. Cut in half at an angle and wrap tightly in whatever you like to transport sandwiches in.

The Conversation Starter

MAKES
1 cocktail

TIME
5 minutes

INGREDIENTS

2 ounces (60 ml) mezcal
1 tablespoon lime or orange juice
A good pinch of regular or smoky flaky salt
Lime or orange wedge, for garnish

My friend Myna and I created and coined this drink during the first summer we had at The Windy Poplars. She prefers flaky smoky salt, while I prefer the original. However, we did agree, regardless of your salt preference, after one drink you'll be talking about having another.

METHOD

Fill a glass of your liking with ice, a small tumbler is usually a good place to start. Pour in the mezcal and stir in the lime juice and the salt. Taste and adjust with more lime juice and salt to taste. Garnish with the lime or orange wedge and start talking.

harman/kardon

Roasted Eggplant Dip *with* Toasted Seeds

SERVES
4 to 6

TIME
1 ½ hours

INGREDIENTS

- 2 large globe eggplants (about 3½ pounds/1.6 kg total)
- 3 tablespoons extra-virgin olive oil, plus some more as needed
- ½ teaspoon cumin seeds
- ½ teaspoon toasted sesame seeds
- 3 tablespoons tahini
- 1 teaspoon ground cumin
- 1 clove garlic, grated
- Juice of 1 lemon, plus more if needed
- Kosher salt
- ¼ teaspoon dried mint
- 2 tablespoons roughly chopped fresh dill, mint, or parsley
- Flaky salt, for serving

I crave Mediterranean food all year-round, but especially in the summer, which is also when eggplants happen to be in season. This dip is my version of baba ghanoush. It's my version because I'm what one would call "a seed girl," which means that if it is tossed, topped, or toasted with *any* sort of seed, I will order it without question and that is what I've done here. I also took the liberty of adding dried mint, which frankly Americans don't use enough of in their cooking and I'm here to change that. Don't get me wrong, I'm a fresh herb fiend, but dried mint offers not only more intense flavor, but also texture. Serve to start with pitas or flatbread and crudités or alongside the Spiced Lamb and Lemon Skewers with Cucumber and Sumac (page 190).

METHOD

Preheat the oven to 425°F (220°C).

Prick the eggplants with a fork all over the skin. Halve the eggplants lengthwise and with your hands slather both sides with some olive oil until coated. Set cut side down on a sheet pan.

Roast until the skin completely collapses, 35 to 40 minutes.

Let cool for 10 to 15 minutes and when you are able to handle them, scrape the flesh over a colander with a bowl underneath, removing any dark browned bits. Let the eggplant sit for 20 minutes or so, so it can release as much moisture as possible.

Meanwhile, in a small dry skillet, toast the cumin seeds and sesame seeds, stirring frequently, until fragrant, 2 to 3 minutes.

Transfer the drained eggplant to a bowl and stir in the 3 tablespoons olive oil, tahini, ground cumin, garlic, lemon juice, and a good pinch of kosher salt. Taste and adjust seasonings as needed with more lemon and salt. Drizzle with some more olive oil and top with the toasted cumin and sesame seeds, dried mint, fresh herbs, and a few pinches of flaky salt.

Snacking Peppers

SERVES
4 to 6

TIME
25 minutes

INGREDIENTS

2 pounds (910 g) small sweet peppers
¼ cup (60 ml) extra-virgin olive oil, plus more for serving
Kosher salt
A few thyme sprigs (optional)
3 ounces (85 g) good-quality feta cheese (I like the French kind, it's creamier)
½ cup (15 g) torn fresh herbs, such as parsley, basil, mint, or cilantro
Flaky salt, for serving

In the summer, it's usually a full house at the farm, and I wouldn't have it any other way. The snacking menu rotates with whatever is in the fridge, but the one thing I always return to is roasted sweet peppers with feta and herbs. They pair well with everything and are gorgeous to look at, making them seem much more complicated to prepare than they actually are. I also love this recipe for its versatility. Sometimes, I will top the peppers with garlic and capers that I have toasted in olive oil. Herbs are also interchangeable—I've used Italian parsley, basil, mint, cilantro, dill, and chives. Sometimes just one, sometimes all together depending on what's around. Plate them on something pretty and call it a day. In fact, when we have no guests coming for a week, I still plan on making them because with the very likely chance that someone pops by, I'll bring the peppers to room temperature, toast some bread, and open a bottle of wine. And snack night begins again.

METHOD

Preheat the oven to 375°F (190°C).

Arrange the peppers on a large sheet pan. Drizzle with the olive oil, season well with salt, and toss to coat. Top with the thyme (if using).

Roast the peppers, turning once, until they collapse and become golden, 20 to 25 minutes.

Transfer the peppers to a platter or shallow bowl and allow them to come to room temperature. When you're ready to serve them, top with the feta cheese, the torn herbs, a good pinch of flaky salt, and a drizzle of olive oil, if you like.

A Note: As I mentioned above, I sometimes like to top these with garlic and capers. If you would, too, thinly slice 3 doves of garlic and heat in a bit of olive oil with a tablespoon or so of drained capers, just until they begin to turn golden. Remove them with a slotted spoon and scatter over the peppers. Then add the feta and herbs.

VEG

Golden *and* Crispy Leeks *with* Melted Gruyère

SERVES
4

TIME
45 minutes

I love a leek and you should, too. I always have them on hand in my "cool pantry"—aka my fridge—for soups and stews and braises. However, they are also wonderful on their own, and when roasted and topped with Gruyère cheese until golden and bubbling, even more so. Serve alongside roast chicken, seared lamb, or pork chops, or a simple green salad and call it dinner.

INGREDIENTS

- 6 medium leeks, white and light-green parts only, trimmed and halved lengthwise
- ⅓ cup (75 ml) extra-virgin olive oil
- Kosher salt and freshly ground black pepper
- 4 thyme sprigs, leaves picked
- 2 ounces (55 g) grated Gruyère cheese
- Grated zest of 1 lemon
- 1 tablespoon thinly sliced fresh chives
- Flaky salt, for serving (optional)

METHOD

Preheat the oven to 425°F (220°C).

Drizzle the leeks with the olive oil and use your hands to thoroughly coat them. Season well with salt and pepper. Arrange the leeks cut side down in a 9 by 13-inch (23 by 33 cm) baking dish.

Roast until they begin to soften, about 20 minutes. Remove from the oven and flip so the leeks are cut side up, and then scatter the Gruyère evenly over the top. Return the leeks to the oven and continue to roast until the cheese has melted and some of the leeks have turned crunchy and golden, 10 to 12 minutes more.

Transfer to a plate or serve right from the pan and scatter the lemon zest and chives over top. Season with flaky salt, if you please.

Butter Rice *with* Roasted Tomatoes *and* Herbs

SERVES
4

TIME
30 minutes

INGREDIENTS

2 pounds (910 g) Campari tomatoes, halved
¼ cup (60 ml) extra-virgin olive oil
Kosher salt and freshly ground black pepper
1 clove garlic, peeled but whole
2¼ cups (540 ml) chicken or vegetable stock
4 tablespoons (56 g/½ stick) butter
1 small yellow onion, finely chopped
1½ cups (285 g) long-grain rice, such as jasmine or basmati, rinsed
½ cup (25 g) roughly chopped mixed fresh herbs, such as basil, dill, mint, and parsley
Flaky salt, for serving

This recipe was a happy accident. Growing up we had rice pilaf fairly often; I mean, what's better than rice toasted in butter and cooked in stock? Not much. I don't make it as much as I'd like, but I always get a resounding "Yes, please!" from Chad when I offer. I happened to have some off-season tomatoes lying about that weren't for eating as they should be eaten (with nothing but salt or on a sandwich with mayonnaise), so I decided to roast them and spoon them on top of the rice. Herbs also come into play, and while you should choose whichever ones you like, I am partial to basil, dill, and mint. Serve alongside roast chicken or fish. I ate it solo in my office for lunch the following day, happy as ever.

METHOD

Preheat the oven to 450°F.

On a sheet pan, toss the tomatoes with the olive oil and season well with salt and pepper. Roast until they begin to collapse and turn golden in spots, about 20 minutes. Remove from the oven and grate the garlic over the tomatoes and set aside.

Meanwhile, in a small saucepan, bring the chicken stock to a boil.

In a small Dutch oven or saucepan with a lid, melt the butter over medium-low heat. Add the onion and cook until it has softened and turned golden, 3 to 4 minutes. Season with salt. Add the rice and stir to coat in the butter, and cook until the rice is slightly toasted, 2 to 3 minutes more.

Pour the stock into the rice and cook for 1 minute at a boil. Reduce the heat to a simmer, cover, and cook until the rice has absorbed the stock and it is cooked through, 11 to 13 minutes. Remove from the heat and let it stand covered for 10 minutes or so.

When ready to serve, arrange the rice on a large plate or platter; top with the tomatoes and spoon over any juices that have accumulated. Scatter with the herbs and a few pinches of flaky salt and take to the table.

Asparagus *with* Chili Crisp Mayo, Lime, *and* Many Herbs

SERVES
4

TIME
15 minutes

INGREDIENTS

Kosher salt

1 bunch asparagus, woody ends snapped off

⅓ cup (75 ml) aioli, homemade (page 229) or store-bought, or mayonnaise

2 tablespoons chili crisp, such as Fly By Jing

1½ tablespoons fresh lime juice, plus more to taste

¼ cup (12 g) roughly chopped fresh herbs, such as chives and their blossoms, basil, cilantro, or mint

Toasted sesame oil, for drizzling

Toasted sesame seeds, for topping

Grated zest of 1 lime

Flaky salt, for serving

When asparagus is in season I tend to eat a lot of it. I first brought this dish next door to my friend Kelly's house for a late-spring BBQ and it's been requested ever since. The asparagus is simply blanched in well-salted water and served atop aioli mixed with chili crisp and some lime juice for acidity. It's topped with lots of herbs and sesame seeds for a nice crunch. Serve at room temperature or with a slight chill, but hold on to the herbs until just before serving so they don't wilt. Pairs well with grilled everything.

METHOD

Bring a large pot of salted water to a boil. Add the asparagus and blanch for 2 to 3 minutes. Remove to a colander and immediately run under cold water to stop the cooking.

In a medium bowl, combine the aioli, chili crisp, lime juice, and a good pinch of salt and stir to combine. The aioli should release and be a bit more spreadable. Taste and season with salt or more lime juice as needed to your liking.

On a platter or plate, take a spoon or spatula and spread the chili crisp mayonnaise in an even layer. Place the asparagus on top and scatter with the herbs.

Drizzle with some toasted sesame oil and top with some sesame seeds and lime zest and a few pinches of flaky salt.

Braised Snap Peas, Lettuces, *and other* Spring Things *in a* Bit of Cream

SERVES
4

TIME
25 minutes

INGREDIENTS

2 tablespoons (28 g) unsalted butter
1 spring onion, finely chopped
3 stalks green garlic, finely chopped, or 2 cloves garlic, finely chopped
1 small fennel bulb, cored and finely chopped
½ cup (120 ml) dry vermouth or white wine
Kosher salt
6 ounces (170 g) sugar snap peas, strings removed and cut on the bias
2 heads Little Gem lettuce, quartered
Freshly ground black pepper
1 cup (240 ml) chicken or vegetable stock
2 tablespoons heavy cream
¼ cup (12g) torn mixed fresh herbs, such as mint, chives, and dill
Grated zest of 1 lemon
Flaky salt, for serving

This simple spring recipe is inspired by a classic dish seen all over menus in France. I've also added fennel, because sometimes I can't help myself and have to lean just a little bit Italian. We often see many gray and cool days come spring and it would be perfect to serve on one of them. It also could serve as a main for two with some toasted bread and lots of butter on the side.

METHOD

In a 12-inch (30 cm) skillet, melt the butter over medium-low heat. Add the spring onion, green garlic, and fennel and cook, stirring occasionally until they have softened, but have not taken on any color, about 3 minutes. Add the vermouth and bring to a boil, lower to a simmer, and cook until reduced by half, 2 minutes or so. Season with salt.

Add the snap peas and lettuce, stir gently to coat in the butter, and cook until the peas turn bright green and the lettuce begins to soften, 2 to 3 minutes. Season with salt and pepper.

Add the stock, bring to a simmer, and cook until reduced by about half, 2 to 3 minutes more. Turn the heat to medium, stir in the cream, and cook until it begins to thicken slightly, about 2 minutes.

Plate the vegetables in a bowl or on a platter. Scatter with the herbs, some of the lemon zest, a pinch or two of flaky salt, and another grind of pepper should you choose. Taste and adjust seasonings with salt and more lemon zest as you like.

Shaved Asparagus Salad *with* Comté, Toasted Almonds, *and* Fried Prosciutto

SERVES
4

TIME
20 minutes

INGREDIENTS

1 bunch asparagus (about 12 ounces/340 g), woody ends snapped off
3 tablespoons extra-virgin olive oil
4 thin slices prosciutto (about 2½ ounces total)
½ cup (70 g) roasted Marcona almonds or regular almonds
Kosher salt and freshly ground black pepper
¾ cup (80 g) shaved cheese, such as Comté, Gruyère, or Parmesan
½ cup (25 g) roughly chopped soft fresh herbs, such as mint, tarragon, or parsley, or a combination
2 tablespoons fresh lemon juice
Flaky salt, for serving

The idea for this recipe came to me in a dream—it happens sometimes! I'm glad it did, and you will be, too. Asparagus is shaved and tossed with cheese, toasted almonds, and fried prosciutto and then tossed with bright lemon juice and olive oil—it hits all the notes you want it to. I've called for Comté cheese, which has been increasingly available in grocery stores, but if you can't find it, feel free to substitute Gruyère; they both offer great nuttiness. If you'd like to make this vegetarian, simply leave out the prosciutto, it's still delicious. This salad is best served in spring when asparagus spears begin popping up at the market.

METHOD

Using a Y-peeler or vegetable peeler, shave the asparagus into long, thin strips (I like to leave most of the tips whole) and transfer to a large bowl and set aside.

Line a plate with paper towels and have near the stove. In a 12-inch (30 cm) skillet, heat 1 tablespoon of the olive oil over medium heat until it shimmers. Add the prosciutto and cook until it is golden and crispy, 2 to 3 minutes. Remove from the skillet and place on the paper towels to drain.

Add the almonds to the pan, toss to coat in the prosciutto oil, and cook, stirring frequently, until toasty and golden, about 3 minutes. Transfer to a cutting board and when cool enough to touch, roughly chopped the nuts. With your hands, tear the prosciutto into bite-size pieces.

Season the asparagus with salt and pepper. Add half the cheese, half the nuts, half the prosciutto, half the herbs, and toss with the remaining 2 tablespoons olive oil and the lemon juice. Taste and adjust with more salt if needed. Top with the remaining cheese, nuts, herbs, and prosciutto.

Roasted Potato Salad *with* Za'atar, Feta, *and* Mint

SERVES
4

TIME
50 minutes

INGREDIENTS

1½ pounds (680 g) baby Yukon Gold potatoes, halved

2 tablespoons extra-virgin olive oil, plus more for drizzling

2 teaspoons za'atar or dried thyme

Kosher salt and freshly ground black pepper

2½ ounces (70 g) feta cheese (I like the French type, which is creamier)

⅓ cup (50 g) pitted and smashed Castelvetrano olives or other olives of your choosing

¼ cup (13 g) torn fresh mint

Flaky salt, for serving

This potato salad decidedly does not need a picnic blanket or an outdoor setting. It's a warm potato salad for cooler weather that should be served at the dining table with a fork and a knife. She's elegant and she's refined, but she's also comforting. Serve with A Very Spiced Chicken with Cippolinis and Preserved Lemon and Date Relish (page 196).

METHOD

Preheat the oven to 425°F (220°C).

Toss the potatoes with the olive oil and za'atar and season well with salt and pepper. Spread on a sheet pan and roast until golden brown, 40 to 45 minutes, tossing halfway through.

Place the potatoes in a medium bowl and toss gently with the feta, olives, and half of the mint. Drizzle with some more olive oil if you like. Top with the remaining mint and season with flaky salt.

Peas, Shoots, and Leaves *with* Buttermilk *and* Feta Dressing

SERVES
4

TIME
15 minutes

INGREDIENTS

¾ cup (180 ml) whole buttermilk
2½ ounces (70 g) crumbled feta cheese (preferably French if you can find it)
5 tablespoons (75 ml) fresh lemon juice (about 2 lemons)
Kosher salt and freshly ground black pepper
8 ounces (225 g) snap peas, cut on the bias
3 scallions, thinly sliced on the bias
2 ounces (55 g) pea shoots
2 tablespoons extra-virgin olive oil, plus more for drizzling
2 tablespoons minced chives and/or blossoms, for scattering
2 tablespoons roughly chopped or torn fresh mint leaves
Flaky salt, for serving

The truth is, I developed this recipe because I always wanted to call something by this name. She's witty, eh? But this salad is also a bit of a showstopper. The tangy buttermilk and feta dressing is best tumbled with peak spring produce, and the snap peas offer a lovely counterbalance to its creaminess with their crunch. Serve it with whatever else you're making for dinner and New Potatoes and Mint with Too Much Butter (page 235) alongside.

METHOD

In a medium bowl, whisk together the buttermilk, feta, and 3 tablespoons of the lemon juice and season well with salt and a good few churns of black pepper. Taste and adjust seasoning with salt as needed. Set aside.

In another bowl, gently toss together the snap peas, scallions, and pea shoots with the remaining 2 tablespoons lemon juice and the olive oil. Season with salt.

To serve, transfer the dressing to a medium plate or platter, preferably with sides, and mound the snap pea mixture on top in the middle. Drizzle with some more olive oil and scatter with the chive blossoms and mint. Finish with a few pinches of flaky salt.

Little Gems *with* Avocado, Pistachios, *and* Miso-Honey Dressing

SERVES
4

TIME
15 minutes

INGREDIENTS

for the dressing:

- 2 tablespoons plus 1 teaspoon white miso
- 2 teaspoons runny honey
- ¼ cup (60 ml) fresh lime juice
- Kosher salt (optional)

for the salad:

- 4 heads Little Gem, leaves separated, or 1 head romaine, torn
- 2 small avocados, cut into ½-inch (12 mm) pieces
- 1 small bunch spring onions/scallions, thinly sliced on the bias
- 3 tablespoons roughly chopped pistachios or store bought or homemade crispy shallots
- Flaky salt, for finishing

Chad will often request a big green salad to go alongside whatever else we're having for dinner. And in my quest never to waste a meal without treating it as a recipe development assignment, this salad was born. We both enjoyed it so much, I made it three times in a week, while also recipe testing the Harissa and Brown Sugar Glazed Salmon (page 178) and I'd happily repeat the process. This dressing is not only delicious with this salad but would also be lovely spooned over roasted or sautéed vegetables, a noodle or grain bowl, or pretty much anything else you can imagine. I don't call for oil in this dressing—you don't need it. The miso provides all the creaminess you're looking for.

METHOD

Make the dressing: In a medium bowl, whisk together the miso, honey, 2 tablespoons water, and the lime juice. Taste, and if needed, season with a bit of kosher salt and set aside.

Assemble the salad: On a large platter, arrange the Little Gem leaves (casually!) starting with the largest ones on the bottom and finishing with the smaller ones on top. If using romaine, simply transfer to the platter.

Scatter the avocado, spring onions, and pistachios evenly over the top of the lettuce. Drizzle with some of the dressing, making sure it gets into the nooks and crannies of the lettuce cups. Taste and add more dressing as needed. Finish with a few pinches of flaky salt.

Roasted Carrots *with* Cilantro Yogurt *and* Roasted Pistachios

SERVES
4 to 6

TIME
30 minutes

INGREDIENTS

for the carrots:

1 ½ pounds (680 g) carrots, peeled and sliced lengthwise

Kosher salt and freshly ground black pepper

1 teaspoon ground coriander

2 tablespoons extra-virgin olive oil

for the cilantro yogurt:

1 cup (240 ml) whole-milk Greek yogurt

½ cup (20 g) finely chopped fresh cilantro

1 jalapeño, finely chopped (seeded if you'd like it less spicy)

¼ teaspoon ground coriander

1 tablespoon fresh lime juice (from about ½ lime)

Kosher salt

for serving:

¼ cup (30 g) finely chopped salted roasted pistachios

3 tablespoons thinly sliced scallion greens

Flaky salt, for serving

Lime wedges, for squeezing

The often-overlooked carrot takes center stage for this gorgeous side. Tangy Greek yogurt is combined with cilantro, finely chopped jalapeño for a bit of heat, ground coriander, and lime juice, to create a creamy landing for carrots that have been roasted until nicely caramelized. Salted roasted pistachios finish the dish, adding a crunchy texture; toasted sunflower seeds would also be nice. If you can find rainbow carrots, this dish becomes even more of a stunner.

METHOD

Preheat the oven to 400°F (200°C).

Roast the carrots: In a large bowl, season the carrots well with salt and pepper. Add the ground coriander and toss the mixture together with the olive oil. Place the carrots cut side down on a sheet pan and roast until golden brown and tender, 25 to 30 minutes, flipping halfway through. Allow to cool slightly.

Meanwhile, make the cilantro yogurt: In a bowl, combine the yogurt, cilantro, jalapeno, ground coriander, lime juice, and a good pinch of salt. Stir well to combine and taste, adjusting seasonings accordingly with more salt and lime as needed.

To serve: Spread the cilantro yogurt on the bottom of a plate or platter and arrange the roasted carrots on top. Scatter with the pistachios and the scallion greens and finish with flaky salt and a squeeze of lime juice.

Tomato Salad *with* Anchovy Bread Crumbs

SERVES
4 to 6

TIME
20 minutes

INGREDIENTS

- 2½ pounds (1.2 kg) heirloom tomatoes, different colors, shapes, and sizes, cut into thin slices or halved as needed for Sungolds and cherry tomatoes
- Flaky salt and freshly ground black pepper
- 2 tablespoons extra-virgin olive oil, plus more for drizzling
- 2 large cloves garlic, finely chopped
- 4 oil-packed anchovy fillets
- 1½ teaspoons crushed fennel seeds
- ½ teaspoon red pepper flakes or 1 fresh cayenne chile, thinly sliced (optional)
- 1 cup (80 g) panko bread crumbs
- 2 teaspoons grated lemon zest, or to taste
- 2 tablespoons Italian parsley leaves
- 2 tablespoons torn basil leaves

Before you ask, yes, you do need another tomato salad and it's this one. It's best made during the peak summer season with lots of tomato varieties, colors, shapes, and sizes for vibrancy. Anchovies and fennel seeds are melted and toasted in olive oil and act as the flavorful base of the toasted crumbs, which are spooned over the tomatoes before showering everything with herbs. Serve with grilled anything and rosé around a picnic table.

METHOD

About 10 minutes before serving, place tomatoes in a large, deep platter or low-sided serving bowl, season with flaky salt and black pepper and drizzle with a good amount of olive oil.

In a medium skillet, combine the 2 tablespoons olive oil, garlic, anchovies, fennel seeds, and pepper flakes (if using). Set over medium heat and cook, stirring occasionally, until the anchovies have melted into the oil, the garlic is fragrant, and the fennel seeds are toasted, 5 to 6 minutes.

Add the panko, toss to coat in the oil, and cook until golden, stirring frequently to make sure they don't burn, about 5 minutes. Remove from the heat and stir in the lemon zest and a pinch of flaky salt. Taste and adjust seasonings with more salt as needed, you likely don't need much as anchovies are salty already.

Spoon the panko over top of the tomatoes and scatter with the herbs.

Tomato, Fennel, *and* White Bean Salad *with* Torn Bread *and* Smoky Aioli

SERVES
3 or 4

TIME
25 minutes

INGREDIENTS

8 ounces (225 g) mixed heirloom regular and cherry tomatoes, cut in half and larger ones cut into chunks

1½ cups (130 g) thinly sliced fennel (from 1 medium bulb)

1 small shallot, thinly sliced into rings

1 can (15 ounces/425 g) butter beans, drained, or 1½ cups (85 g) cooked beans

5 tablespoons (75 ml) extra-virgin olive oil, plus more for drizzling

Kosher salt and freshly ground black pepper

6 ounces (170 g) rustic bread, torn into 1-inch (2.5 cm) pieces

½ cup (120 ml) Immersion Blender Aioli (page 229) or mayonnaise

1½ teaspoons 'nduja

Small fistful of basil, torn

Flaky salt, for serving

If you're a smart summer shopper, you'll likely have most of these ingredients within close reach. For your sake, I hope you do, as this is a very, very good salad. I have a tendency to make a lot of aioli during the summer; it pairs well with everything and it's a small luxury to have lying around waiting for ways to be used up. I also usually happen to have 'nduja in the fridge as we frequently use it as a pizza topping (page 144). If you don't, smoked paprika will work well in its place. I like to serve this recipe with the Pan-Seared Butter-Basted Sesame Scallops (page 158).

METHOD

In a large bowl, gently toss together the tomatoes, fennel, shallot, beans, 2 tablespoons of the olive oil, a good pinch of kosher salt, and a few grinds of black pepper. Set aside.

In a 12-inch (30 cm) skillet, heat the remaining 3 tablespoons olive oil over medium heat until it shimmers. Add the torn bread and cook, stirring occasionally, until the bread is toasty and golden, 5 to 7 minutes. Remove from the heat and cool slightly.

Meanwhile, mix together the aioli and the 'nduja until well combined. Take a spoon or a spatula and swoosh the mixture onto a large plate or platter.

Toss the toasted bread with the tomato and fennel mixture. The tomatoes will have released a fair amount of juice to coat everything nicely. Taste and season with more salt and pepper as needed. Pile on top of the smoky aioli. Top with the basil, some more olive oil, and a few pinches of flaky salt.

Summer Squash Salad *with* Toasted Pine Nuts *and* Blue Cheese

SERVES
4

TIME
40 minutes

INGREDIENTS

- 4 tablespoons (60 ml) extra-virgin olive oil
- 2 pounds (910 g) assorted zucchini and summer squash, cut into rounds ¼ inch (6 mm) thick
- Kosher salt and freshly ground black pepper
- 1½ tablespoons pine nuts
- Grated zest of 1 lemon
- 2 ounces (55 g) good-quality blue cheese
- Small fistful of basil, torn

On a late-August afternoon, our friends Scott, Alice, and their daughter Vera came by for a visit and a swim, and of course I felt the need to put out snacks. As one is usually overwhelmed by the amount of zucchini piling up (myself included), I wanted to utilize it, but also make it feel special. I did so by sautéing it until golden and topping the zucchini with toasted nuts and crumbly cheese, and as it was summer, clearly a showering of basil was necessary. The squash can be fried and left at room temperature earlier in the day, but I would wait to garnish it until just before serving. One of my favorite ways to entertain this time of year is to make a number of vegetable salads such as this that can be served at room temperature. When guests arrive, all you need to do is fire up the grill and cook one thing, be it fish, steak, or otherwise and let the sides steal the show. They've waited all year to do so, so let them enjoy their time.

METHOD

Line a plate with paper towels and have near the stove. In a 12-inch (30 cm) skillet, heat 2 tablespoons of the oil over medium heat until it shimmers. Working in batches so as to not crowd the pan, add about half of the squash and cook, flipping frequently, until it begins to soften and turn golden in spots, 5 to 8 minutes. Season with salt and pepper. Transfer the squash to the paper towels to drain. Repeat with the remaining 2 tablespoons oil and remaining squash.

While the squash cooks, heat a small skillet over medium heat. Add the pine nuts and toast, stirring often, until they are aromatic and golden in spots, 3 to 4 minutes. Transfer to a small bowl.

Transfer the squash to a platter and top with the lemon zest and pine nuts, and scatter with the blue cheese and the basil. Taste and adjust seasonings with more salt if needed.

Fresh Corn Polenta *with* Green Chiles *and* Coconut Milk

SERVES
4

TIME
20 minutes

INGREDIENTS

8 ears corn, shucked

3 tablespoons canola, grapeseed, or other neutral oil

2 to 3 Thai green chiles, finely chopped

3 scallions, thinly sliced, white and dark green parts kept separate

¾ cup (180 ml) full-fat coconut milk

Kosher salt and freshly ground black pepper

½ lime, for squeezing

¼ cup (10 g) roughly chopped fresh cilantro, both leaves and tender stems

Flaky salt, for serving

My friend Ali Stafford, author of *Pizza Night*, is responsible for turning me into a fresh corn polenta nut. She posted a recipe on her website years ago and I've been making it ever since. There is no better late-summer corn recipe, and this dish is worth the wait! I took the liberty of making it my own by adding spicy chiles and coconut milk for even more creaminess. I'd serve this alongside simply grilled shrimp or scallops.

METHOD

Working over a large bowl, grate the kernels off of the cob on the large holes of a box grater. You will be left with a wet, soupy consistency. That is okay.

In a 12-inch (30 cm) skillet, heat the oil over medium heat. Add the chiles and scallion whites and cook, stirring frequently, until softened, 2 to 3 minutes.

Add the corn and coconut milk and simmer until it begins to slightly thicken, 5 to 7 minutes. Season with salt and freshly ground pepper. Take off the heat and allow it to sit a few minutes more, if needed, to thicken additionally.

Stir in a good squeeze of lime juice. Taste and adjust with more salt or lime juice as needed.

Transfer to a medium bowl and top with the scallion greens and cilantro and a few pinches of flaky salt.

Smoky Toasted Corn Salad *with* Fried Shallots

SERVES
4

TIME
20 minutes

INGREDIENTS

- 2 tablespoons neutral oil, such as canola or vegetable
- 5 ears corn, kernels removed
- 3 ounces (85 g) 'nduja (optional)
- 2 cloves garlic, finely chopped
- ⅓ cup (40 g) thinly sliced white onion
- Grated zest and juice of ½ lime
- Kosher salt
- ¼ cup (13 g) roughly chopped or torn fresh mint and basil
- Fried shallots, homemade (page 233) or store-bought, for garnish

This summer salad is equally good served warm as it is room temperature and travels well, should you be potlucking or picnicking. The sweetness of the corn plays nicely with the smoky, spiciness of the 'nduja, while getting a nice lift from the lime, and a good crunch from the fried shallots. Should you want to make this vegetarian, swap the 'nduja for a teaspoon or two of smoked paprika. If you are taking her on the road, I'd pack the shallots separately and top the dish right before serving so they maintain their crispiness.

METHOD

In a 12-inch (30 cm) skillet, heat the oil over medium heat until it shimmers. Add the corn and cook, stirring occasionally, until it begins to turn brown and golden in spots, 4 to 6 minutes.

Add the 'nduja (if using) and stir until it has melted into the corn and slightly begins to crisp, 3 minutes or so. Add the garlic and cook for 1 minute more until fragrant.

Remove the pan from the heat and stir in the white onion, lime zest, and lime juice and season to taste with salt.

Transfer the corn to a platter and top with the herbs and the fried shallots. Taste and adjust the seasoning with more lime juice and salt if needed.

Crunchy Celery *and* Scallion Salad *with* Blue Cheese *and* Marcona Almonds

SERVES
4

TIME
15 minutes

INGREDIENTS

- 1 bunch celery, about 10 stalks, with their leaves, sliced 2 inches (5 cm) on the bias
- 1 medium bunch scallions, sliced 2 inches (5 cm) on the bias
- 4 ounces (115 g) good-quality blue cheese, crumbled
- ½ cup (65 g) chopped Marcona or toasted regular almonds
- 2 tablespoons fresh lemon juice, plus more as needed
- 2 tablespoons extra-virgin olive oil, plus more as needed
- Kosher salt and freshly ground black pepper
- Flaky salt, for serving

This recipe is inspired by a Gabrielle Hamilton dish where she serves blue cheese toasts topped with a celery salad. I made it for my birthday a few years ago for the grazing portion of the evening and it was a big hit. It got me thinking that its components would be a beautiful standalone salad as well. I added Marcona almonds for crunch, but if you can't find them, toast regular almonds in a skillet over medium heat until golden and chop them up instead. As there are few ingredients, using a good-quality blue cheese is highly recommended. I like Rogue River Blue from Oregon or Jasper Hill Farm's Withersbrook Blue. Serve alongside pretty much anything grilled or roasted.

METHOD

In a large bowl, combine the celery, scallions, half the blue cheese, and half the almonds. Add the lemon juice, olive oil, and season with salt and pepper. Toss together. Taste and adjust seasonings with more lemon juice, olive, and salt to your liking.

Serve topped with the remaining cheese and nuts and a few pinches of flaky salt.

Snappy *and* Herby Potato Salad *with* Frizzled Leeks

SERVES
6 to 8

TIME
30 minutes

INGREDIENTS

2 pounds (910 g) Yukon Gold potatoes
½ cup (67 g) kosher salt
1 cup (90 g) thinly sliced fennel
2 celery stalks, thinly sliced
2 stalks green garlic, thinly sliced, or 2 cloves garlic, grated
2 spring onions or 3 scallions, thinly sliced
1 cup (50 g) roughly chopped tender fresh herbs, such as mint and parsley
3 tablespoons Dijon mustard
3 tablespoons extra-virgin olive oil, plus more as needed
¼ cup (60 ml) fresh lemon juice (about 2 lemons)
Freshly ground black pepper

for the frizzled leeks:
3 tablespoons grapeseed oil
1 medium leek, white and light-green parts only, rinsed and sliced into ¼-inch rounds
Flaky salt, for finishing

Unlike its sophisticated older cousin (page 66), this potato salad begs for warmer weather and possibly a beach blanket. The combination of the tender boiled potatoes with the raw crunchy fennel and celery offers a lovely contrast in textures, and the mustard dressing gives it lovely zip. This dish can be made a day or two in advance without the herbs if you'd like to get ahead of things. Bring to room temperature before doing so, stir in the herbs, and top with the frizzled leeks right before serving.

METHOD

In a large soup pot or Dutch oven, combine the potatoes and enough water to cover the potatoes by 1 inch. Add the salt, bring to a boil, and cook until the potatoes are tender and easily pierced by a fork, 10 to 15 minutes.

Drain the potatoes and when cool enough to handle, roughly chop them.

In a large bowl, combine the potatoes, fennel, celery, green garlic, spring onions, herbs, mustard, olive oil, and lemon juice. Season very well with salt and a few grinds of black pepper. Toss together gently until well combined, taste and adjust seasonings as needed with salt and more oil if needed.

Meanwhile, make the frizzled leeks: Line a plate with paper towels and have near the stove. In a 12-inch (30 cm) skillet, heat the oil over high heat until it shimmers. Add the leeks and cook, stirring occasionally, until crispy and golden, 3 to 5 minutes. With a spider strainer or slotted spoon, carefully transfer the leeks onto the paper towels and sprinkle with flaky salt.

Refrigerate the potato salad until you're ready to serve and finish with a few pinches of flaky salt and a generous handful of frizzled leeks.

Fennel Gratin *with* Olives *and* Provolone

SERVES
4 to 6

TIME
1 hour

INGREDIENTS

1½ pounds (680 g) fennel (about 2 medium), thinly sliced lengthwise

1 large shallot, thinly sliced

12 Castelvetrano olives, crushed and pitted

Kosher salt and freshly ground black pepper

1 cup (240 ml) heavy cream

½ cup (55 g) freshly grated extra-sharp provolone cheese

¼ cup (60 ml) chicken stock or vegetables stock

for the topping:

¾ cup (60 g) panko bread crumbs

1 tablespoon fennel seeds, pounded in a mortar and pestle or finely chopped

1 teaspoon grated lemon zest

1 teaspoon red pepper flakes

¼ cup (25 g) grated Pecorino Romano cheese

2 cloves garlic, grated

3 tablespoons extra-virgin olive oil

Is there anything better than a gratin? No, there is not. This one makes for a perfect side on a cold night and is studded with buttery green olives and laced with salty, sharp provolone. Serve with roasted sausages or chicken. It's also lovely on its own with a big green salad of arugula tossed with lemon juice and good olive oil. If you somehow have leftovers, they would be perfect served with a fried egg on top.

METHOD

Preheat the oven to 375°F (190°C).

In a large bowl, combine the fennel, shallot, olives, and salt and pepper to taste and toss to combine. Transfer to a gratin dish, where everything can fit together snugly. Using the same bowl, mix together the cream, provolone, and chicken stock and pour over the top of the fennel mixture. Cover tightly with foil.

Bake until the fennel is tender, but still has some bite, 35 to 40 minutes. Remove from the oven and turn the heat to 425°F (220°C).

Meanwhile, make the topping: In a medium bowl, stir together the panko, fennel seeds, lemon zest, pepper flakes, pecorino, garlic, and olive oil.

Spoon over top of the fennel. Return to the oven and cook until the top is brown and golden, 20 to 25 minutes. Serve warm.

STAUB

CHAPTER 3

IN BOWLS

An Excellent Lentil Stew *with* Pork, Crispy Walnuts, *and* Lemon

SERVES
4 to 6

TIME
1 hour

Save this stew for a frigid night when the produce shelf looks bleak and leaving the house feels daunting. It is absolutely delicious and as comforting as can be. If you can make it a few hours ahead, do, as it will intensify the flavor of the stew. That said, the lentils will continue to absorb liquid as the stew sits, so it will need a cup or so of water or broth to help loosen it up when you're reheating it to serve. The walnut lemon topping adds a nice, bright crunch, and an extra drizzle of good olive oil is not necessary, but awfully nice.

INGREDIENTS

2 tablespoons extra-virgin olive oil
1 pound (455 g) ground pork (see Note), at room temperature
Kosher salt
1 medium onion, finely chopped
1 small fennel bulb, finely chopped
2 stalks celery, thinly sliced
6 cloves garlic, roughly chopped
1 tablespoon ground fennel seeds
2 rosemary sprigs, leaves picked and finely chopped
½ teaspoon red pepper flakes
1 tablespoon tomato paste
½ cup (120 g) canned crushed tomatoes
2 cups (380 g) brown lentils, rinsed
6 cups (1.4 L) chicken stock

for the walnut lemon topping:
½ cup (60 g) finely chopped walnuts
1 cup (50 g) roughly chopped fresh Italian parsley, both leaves and tender stems
2 tablespoons grated lemon zest (save 1 lemon for serving)
Flaky salt

for serving:
1 lemon, halved
Freshly ground black pepper
Grated pecorino or Parmesan
Olive oil, for drizzling
Good bread, toasted

METHOD

In a large Dutch oven, heat the oil over medium-high heat until it shimmers. Add the pork in an even layer making sure it gets as much contact with the bottom of the pan as possible. Leave the pork alone until you begin to see it browning around the edges. Using a spatula or wooden spoon, begin breaking and flipping the meat to brown the other side, so each side is equally golden and crispy, 10 to 12 minutes total. Season very well with salt.

Reduce the heat to medium, add the onion, fresh fennel, and celery and cook, stirring frequently, until the onion and fennel start to slightly caramelize, 5 to 7 minutes more.

Add the garlic, fennel seeds, rosemary, pepper flakes, and tomato paste and cook for 1 minute more.

Add the crushed tomatoes, lentils, and stock and bring to a boil. Turn down to a gentle simmer, cover with the lid askew, and cook until the lentils are tender, 40 to 45 minutes. Taste and adjust seasoning with salt as needed.

Meanwhile, make the walnut lemon topping: In a large skillet, toast the walnuts over medium-low heat, stirring frequently to ensure that they don't burn, 4 to 5 minutes. Transfer the toasted walnuts to a medium bowl. Add the parsley and lemon zest and toss to coat. Season with flaky salt.

To serve: Ladle the stew into deep bowls and top with some of the walnut lemon mixture and a good squeeze of lemon juice. Pass a pepper mill and grated pecorino or Parmesan at the table and drizzle more olive oil on top should you like.

A Note: Feel free to swap in ground chicken or turkey, preferably dark meat, for the pork.

Simplest Potato *and* Leek Soup *with* Blue Cheese Toasts

SERVES
4

TIME
30 minutes

INGREDIENTS

- 2 tablespoons extra-virgin olive oil
- 2 tablespoons (30 g) butter
- 2 medium leeks (including the dark green tops), thinly sliced and rinsed of grit
- Kosher salt
- 4 cloves garlic, finely chopped
- 1 tablespoon fresh thyme
- ½ cup (120 ml) dry white wine or vermouth
- 5 cups (1.2 L) chicken or vegetable stock
- 1½ pounds (680 g) Yukon Gold or other thin-skinned potatoes, cut into ½-inch (12 mm) cubes
- 1 bay leaf
- ⅓ cup (80 ml) heavy cream
- Freshly ground black pepper

for serving:

- ¼ cup (13 g) roughly chopped mixed fresh herbs, such as dill, parsley, and scallions
- Flaky salt and freshly ground black pepper
- Toasted bread
- Very good blue cheese, such as Stilton or Jasper Hill Bayley Hazen

This soup is particularly good on a blustery evening; it is also very good when you're feeling lazy, but want something comforting to eat, preferably served in deep bowls. A more refined version of this soup calls for you to puree it, and in the summer the French call it Vichyssoise and serve it chilled. This is not that. This is your scrappy, younger, and cooler cousin's version, who doesn't own a blender, but does have a potato masher from Ikea in her overcrowded kitchen drawer. Toast some crusty bread and put a large and good piece of blue cheese out on the table (on a pretty plate) so things can still feel a bit dignified. Fine, *un peu* French.

METHOD

In a large Dutch oven or soup pot, heat the oil and melt the butter over medium heat. Add the leeks and cook, stirring occasionally, until they are soft and translucent, 7 to 10 minutes.

Season with salt. Stir in the garlic and thyme and cook until fragrant, about 1 minute more. Add the white wine, bring to a simmer, and cook until reduced by half, 2 minutes or so.

Add the stock, potatoes, bay leaf, and a large pinch of salt. Cover with the lid slightly askew and bring to a boil, then lower the heat and simmer until the potatoes are falling apart tender, about 20 minutes.

Remove from the heat and discard the bay leaf. With a potato masher, gently push down on the potatoes until they collapse. Some will remain more intact than others, that's okay. You're looking for an almost sludge-like (in the very best way) texture. Stir in the heavy cream. Taste and adjust seasonings with salt as needed and a few generous turns of black pepper.

To serve: Ladle into bowls and top with the herbs and more black pepper and a pinch of flaky salt. Serve with toasted bread and blue cheese at the table.

Cappelletti *in* Brodo *with* Mortadella Meatballs

SERVES
4

TIME
30 minutes

INGREDIENTS
for the meatballs:
4 ounces (115 g) mortadella, roughly chopped
4 ounces (115 g) prosciutto, roughly chopped
8 ounces (225 g) ground pork
Nutmeg
¼ cup (13 g) finely chopped fresh Italian parsley
½ cup (40 g) panko bread crumbs
1 large egg
½ cup (50 g) grated pecorino cheese

for the soup:
6 cups (1.4 L) low-sodium chicken broth
6 ounces (170 g) dried cappelletti pasta
Chopped parsley, for garnish
Grated pecorino, for serving
Freshly ground black pepper

After a long, rewarding day making tortellini in brodo with my dear friend Steph, we both agreed the leftover stuffing would make great meatballs. It got me thinking . . . What if I was to turn the recipe upside down and instead of making freshly stuffed pasta, make the meatballs the star of the show and serve them in broth with small pasta? I did, and it is a winner—not to mention a whole lot less of a lift. If you don't want to make the soup, make the meatballs anyway! They'd be delightful tossed in a red tomato sauce and served on their own or with spaghetti. They also freeze very well should you want to batch them ahead of time.

METHOD

Make the meatballs: Preheat the oven to 425°F (220°C). Line a sheet pan with parchment paper.

In a food processor, combine the mortadella and prosciutto and pulse until it has a similar consistency to the ground pork.

In a large bowl, combine the mortadella/prosciutto mixture, ground pork, nutmeg, parsley, panko, egg, and pecorino. With your hands or a large spoon, mix together until everything is well combined. With damp hands, roll the pork mixture into balls ¾ to 1 inch (2 to 2.5 cm) in diameter; it should yield about 20 meatballs.

Place the meatballs on the lined pan and bake until they are cooked through, about 12 minutes, flipping halfway through to ensure both sides get golden brown. (Alternatively, you could pan-fry these in olive oil, but I don't. I'm a lazy cook and prefer this tidier version.)

Meanwhile, for the soup: In a pot, bring the stock to a boil. Add the pasta and cook according to package directions, stirring frequently to ensure it's not sticking to the bottom of the pot.

Divide the meatballs among bowls and ladle the broth and pasta over top. Sprinkle a bit of parsley over each serving and pass more pecorino at the table. Finish with a few good turns of black pepper.

New Year's Day Ham Soup *with* White Beans *and* Cabbage

SERVES
8

TIME
1½ hours

INGREDIENTS
for the broth:
- 3 tablespoons extra-virgin olive oil
- 1 large leek (including the dark green tops), thinly sliced
- 2 stalks celery, thinly sliced
- 1 medium fennel bulb, roughly chopped
- Kosher salt
- 8 cloves garlic, roughly chopped
- 3 thyme sprigs, leaves picked
- ½ teaspoon red pepper flakes
- 1 ham bone
- 1 bay leaf

for the soup:
- 2 cans (15 ounces/425 g each) butter beans, drained, or 3 cups (510 g) cooked beans
- ½ medium head green savoy or regular cabbage, shredded
- 2 to 3 tablespoons fresh lemon juice (1 to 2 lemons)
- Kosher salt
- Grated Parmesan or pecorino, for serving
- Flaky salt and freshly ground black pepper

For the last few years, my dear friend and nextdoor neighbor, Kelly, has hosted a very fun Open House on New Year's Day. The day consists of pitchers of Bloody Marys, bagels with lox and all the fixings, cheese and meats, and lots of wine. The first year, I could tell that things were getting a bit out of hand and that soup was needed to keep things from getting derailed, so I popped home and pulled together a clean-out-the-fridge with the ham bone from Christmas. It saved people and was therefore requested again, so in turn it became a tradition, which I now make every year—and now you can, too. The ham bone flavors the broth so beautifully, leaving behind a slightly smoky, sweet flavor. I love using butter beans, but cannellinis would also work. Savoy cabbage is also suggested, but another sturdy green, such as lacinato kale or escarole, would be lovely.

METHOD

Build your broth: In a large Dutch oven or heavy-bottomed soup pot, heat the olive oil over medium heat until it shimmers. Add the leek, celery, and fennel and season with salt. Cook, stirring occasionally, until softened, but not taking on any color, 4 to 5 minutes. Add the garlic, thyme, and pepper flakes and cook for 1 minute more. Add the ham bone, 10 cups (2.4 L) of water, and the bay leaf and bring to a boil. Reduce to a simmer, cover, and cook for 1 to 1½ hours, until the broth is fragrant and the flavors have gotten acquainted. Taste and adjust seasonings as needed with salt.

Assemble the soup: When ready to serve, remove the ham from the broth and with tongs remove and shred any meat still left on the bone and return it to the pot. (And if you have more ham in the fridge, you can add that, too.) Discard the bone.

Add the beans and simmer over low heat for 10 minutes more. Add in the cabbage and cook until it just wilts but maintains some of its crunch, 4 to 5 minutes more.

Stir in the lemon juice and adjust the seasonings with salt as needed. Ladle into bowls and top each portion with the Parmesan or pecorino and a few good turns of black pepper and flaky salt.

Chicken and Rice Soup *with* Snap Peas *and* Lots of Ginger

SERVES
4

TIME
40 minutes

INGREDIENTS

3 tablespoons neutral oil, such as canola or vegetable oil
6 scallions, thinly sliced, white and light-green parts kept separate, some dark green parts reserved for garnish
5 cloves garlic, thinly sliced
1 (3-inch/7.5 cm) piece fresh ginger, julienned
2 to 3 Thai bird's eye chiles, thinly sliced, or ½ to 1 teaspoon red pepper flakes
Kosher salt
5 cups (1.2 L) chicken broth
1 pound (455 g) boneless, skinless chicken thighs
1 cup (185 g) long-grain white rice
2 tablespoons soy sauce
8 ounces (225 g) sugar snap peas, thinly sliced on the bias

for serving:
Scallions
Lime wedges
Chili crisp

This soup works nicely in early spring, when the light begins to last longer into the evening but there is still a chill in the air. It will also cure whatever ails you thanks to the addition of plentiful amounts of ginger, garlic, and Thai chiles. It's also incredibly straightforward to put together, as everything happens in one pot. Feel free to swap out snap peas for snow peas or even string beans, should they be in closer reach. A big bunch of pea shoots stirred in right at the end would also be lovely.

METHOD

In a large soup pot or Dutch oven, heat the oil over medium heat until it shimmers. Add the scallions, garlic, ginger, and chiles. Cook, stirring occasionally, until they soften, but take on no real color, 4 to 6 minutes. Season with salt.

Add the chicken broth, chicken thighs, and rice and season with salt. Increase the heat to medium-high and bring to a rapid simmer. Reduce to a low simmer and cook until the chicken is cooked through and the rice is toothsome, 20 to 30 minutes.

Using tongs, remove the chicken from the pot and transfer to a medium bowl or plate. Shred the chicken into pieces, then stir it back into the soup along with the soy sauce and snap peas and cook for 2 minutes more, until the snap peas are just cooked through. Taste and adjust seasonings accordingly with salt.

To serve: Ladle into bowls and top with scallions, a squeeze of lime, and a spoonful of chile crisp.

Chickpea Fennel Stew *with* Swiss Chard *and* Fried Lemon

SERVES
4 to 6

TIME
30 minutes

INGREDIENTS

3 tablespoons extra-virgin olive oil
1 yellow onion, chopped
1 medium fennel bulb, cored and chopped
4 large cloves garlic, roughly chopped
Kosher salt
2 teaspoons dried mint
2 teaspoons ground fennel seeds
2 tablespoons preserved lemon paste
5 cups (1.2 L) vegetable or chicken stock
1 pound (455 g) baby or new potatoes, quartered
2 cans (15.5 ounces/439 g each) chickpeas, drained and rinsed, or 3 cups cooked beans

for the fried lemon:

2 tablespoons extra-virgin olive oil
1 lemon, thinly sliced and seeds removed

to finish:

5 cups (150 g) chopped Swiss chard, with stems
¼ cup (13 g) fresh mint, roughly chopped
Fried shallots (optional), homemade (page 233) or store-bought
Whole-milk Greek yogurt or sour cream (optional)
Flaky salt

This punchy and comforting stew relies heavily on pantry ingredients and your spice drawer and comes together in about 30 minutes. The recipe calls for preserved lemon paste, which provides a bright, floral note, but if paste is not available, feel free to finely chop a preserved one—use about half a lemon. I call for Swiss chard, but lacinato kale, mustard greens, or spinach also work well. Soups and stews are all about toppings, and this one calls for homemade or store-bought fried shallots and Greek yogurt and, while optional, they are recommended for the ultimate spoon-to-sip experience.

METHOD

Heat a large Dutch oven over medium-low heat. Add the olive oil and when it shimmers, add the onion and fresh fennel and cook, stirring often, until softened, about 6 minutes. Add the garlic and cook 1 minute more. Season with salt.

Add the dried mint and fennel seeds and toast the spices in the oil, 1 to 2 minutes more. Stir in the preserved lemon paste.

Add the stock, potatoes, and chickpeas and bring to a steady simmer. Cook until the potatoes are tender, 15 to 20 minutes.

While the stew cooks, make the fried lemon: Heat a medium skillet over medium heat. Add the olive oil and when it shimmers, add the lemon slices. Cook, turning frequently until golden brown, 1 to 2 minutes. Transfer to a cutting board and when cool enough to touch, roughly chop the lemon.

To finish the soup: When the potatoes are tender, use the back of a spatula or potato masher to break down some of the potatoes and the chickpeas to thicken the stew, about ½ cup (120 ml) or so. Add the Swiss chard and cook until the stems have softened and the leaves have wilted, about 4 minutes.

Ladle into bowls and top with fried lemons and the mint. If desired, top with the fried shallots and yogurt. Finish with a few pinches of flaky salt.

Soupy, Sesame Pork Noodles *with* Broccolini *and* Pea Shoots

SERVES
4

TIME
30 minutes

INGREDIENTS

- 2 teaspoons fennel seeds
- 2 tablespoons toasted sesame seeds
- 2 tablespoons neutral oil, such as grapeseed or canola
- 1 pound (455 g) ground pork (see Note)
- Kosher salt
- 1½ cups (175 g) thinly sliced white onion
- 6 cloves garlic, roughly chopped
- 1 tablespoon grated fresh ginger
- 1 teaspoon red pepper flakes
- 6 cups (1.4 L) chicken stock (low sodium if store-bought)
- 3 tablespoons soy sauce
- 1 tablespoon toasted sesame oil
- 1 tablespoon black vinegar or rice wine vinegar
- 6 ounces broccolini, cut into ½-inch (12 mm) pieces
- 8 ounces (225 g) fresh ramen or other long noodles
- 4 cups (80 g) pea shoots or baby spinach

for serving:

- Roughly chopped fresh cilantro
- Thinly sliced white onion
- Toasted sesame seeds
- Chili crisp

This is what I crave when I want something spicy, cozy, and comforting, which if I'm being honest, is pretty much all the time sans peak summer. In addition to the usual aromatics—onion, garlic, ginger—I also add a spice-like paste made of pounded sesame and fennel seeds for depth of flavor. They get briefly toasted in oil before the broth is added. Don't skip this step, it really does add incredible flavor.

METHOD

In a mortar and pestle, pound the fennel and the sesame seeds until they form an almost paste-like consistency and set aside.

In a large Dutch oven or soup pot, heat the neutral oil over medium-high heat until it shimmers. Add the pork in one layer, pressing it down with the back of a spatula or wooden spoon, and cook without moving until it becomes crispy, about 4 minutes. Flip and cook, breaking up the meat until it is no longer pink, 3 to 4 minutes longer. Season with salt, remove with a slotted spoon, and place on a plate.

Reduce the heat to medium and add the onion, adding a bit more oil if needed, depending how lean your pork is. Cook until translucent, about 2 minutes. Add the garlic, ginger, pepper flakes, and the fennel and sesame seed paste and cook 1 minute more. Season with salt.

Stir the pork back in and add the chicken stock, soy sauce, sesame oil, and vinegar. Bring to a simmer and cook for around 20 minutes so the flavors can get to know each other. Add the broccolini and cook until crisp-tender, about 3 minutes.

While the soup simmers, in a separate pot, cook the noodles according to the package directions. Drain and evenly divide the noodles into large soup bowls.

Add the pea shoots to the broth and toss them just to wilt. Spoon some of the pork and broth into each bowl and top with the cilantro, onion, and sesame seeds. A good spoonful of chili crisp would also be nice.

A Note: Should you not eat pork, feel free to swap in chicken or turkey, preferably dark meat if using.

Opening The Windy Poplars

One late spring, on a whim, Chad and I packed up our backpacks (along with five large tote bags full of pantry ingredients and wine glasses—necessities) and headed east to Nova Scotia for a long weekend. Given the house isn't insulated and it's an eleven-hour drive, we hadn't been back since the previous summer, our first, when Hurricane Fiona had claimed a handful of the eighty-foot-tall windy poplars that lined the front of the house. I had come to affectionately call the house "The Windy Poplars," as a nod to my love of the Anne of Green Gables book series, which takes place the next province over, on Prince Edward Island, and has a similar landscape to ours. The farmhouse, built in 1866, also looks not dissimilar. The loss of the trees among other big losses that summer were significant to me and had left me feeling not quite whole.

For some reason, it hadn't occurred to me until we started our journey to Nova Scotia that, schedules permitting, we could go to the house whenever we wanted. This might sound counterintuitive as it is our home, but the comings and goings of having a summer cottage were unfamiliar to me. We had not yet found our rhythm.

I had never been in charge of opening a home for the season or any other time of year for that matter. I had simply only lived in one full-time. The idea of the act, however, gave me an air of great responsibility and maturity. "We are going to open the house," I said confidently and casually to friends without really knowing exactly what it meant, but focusing instead on how good it felt to say. When romanticized, "a house to open" sounded promising and adventurous. It makes me want to reach for an

artisan-looking broom to beat the rugs and clear the cobwebs and cook something nourishing best eaten in bowls with spoons.

The truth was, I had no idea what we were walking into and amid the excitement of figuring it all out, I also held resistance and vulnerability about returning. We had lost Joshie, our nearly twenty-year-old dog, the previous summer; we lived through a terrifying storm, and my mental health, which had taken a very bad turn earlier in the year, was close to being back. But I wasn't fully there yet. What would this year hold? Would I regress into the deep grief of losing Joshie in the spot where he left us? Would my brain start malfunctioning and looping again? Would we be tested again with another storm? Or had we already put our "time in" for an advance return of an uneventful few summers? I was hoping for the latter.

We arrived late on a Wednesday afternoon with a sliver of daylight that Chad very much needed to turn the water back on. The pipes are located in the crumbling basement with no electricity.

Note #1 on the list I'd make for next year would say: "Arrive in time for plenty of daylight!"

Note #2 would read: "Do not hide the keys to the basement door so well you forgot where you hid them!" Which added an extra 30 minutes or so when trying to turn the water on, racing dusk all the while.

As well, two small mice sadly laid in opposite corners of the kitchen in similar situations, creating a minefield of dead black house flies throughout the house.

Note #3 will say: "Do not set mouse traps! The fly carnage outweighs the inevitable outcome of unwilling, sacrificial, and adorable rodents!"

The power had also gone out at some point over the last eight months, so the minimal items we had left in the fridge were no longer and a small amount of filmy gray mold grew in the freezer.

Note #4: "Empty fridge and freezer completely, unplug and leave doors open!"

Note #5 would say: "Remember to be gentle with yourself. You loved that dog more than anything else in the entire world. The grief and pain you hold will shift and change and occasionally still knock the wind out of you. It will be with you forever and you'll carry it with you to any house you are lucky enough to open."

I'm sure this list will continue to evolve.

Around 10 p.m., after the water was running clear, the mold had been bleached away, and the flies were swept up with Chad's shop-vac (no fancy broom available, unfortunately), we opened a bottle of mediocre wine, sat down on the couch, and both let out a big sigh. As inaugural events go, this one was pleasantly successful. I might even trepidatiously say it was "uneventful."

Sweet Corn *and* New Potato Chowder *with* Crab

SERVES
4 to 6

TIME
40 minutes

INGREDIENTS

- 4 tablespoons (60 g) unsalted butter
- ½ white onion, finely chopped
- 2 jalapeños, finely chopped
- 2 celery stalks, finely chopped
- Kosher salt and freshly ground black pepper
- 1¼ pounds (570 g) new potatoes or Yukon Golds, cut into ¼-inch (6 mm) dice
- 4 ears corn, kernels removed
- 4 cups (960 ml) chicken stock
- 2 cups (480 ml) heavy cream
- ½ pound (225 g) lump crabmeat

for serving (optional):

- Thinly sliced scallions
- Basil
- Roughly chopped corn nuts

My friend artist Deanne Fitzpatrick and I once drove an hour and then some to buy late-summer corn in New Brunswick. We had planned to spend the day together shopping for snow crab, good tomatoes, and flaky biscuits, and after being tipped off in the bakery line as to where the best corn was, we hopped in the car without a second thought and were rewarded with incredibly sweet ears of gold. I love having friends that love adventures for food as much as I do. Given the early September weather, the corn beckoned to be cooked with some potatoes in cream. I like topping each portion with a bit of crab if you can find it, but it's just as good without. Serve with Seeded Drop Biscuits (page 218).

METHOD

In a soup pot or large Dutch oven, melt the butter over medium heat. Add the onion, jalapeños, and celery and season well with salt and pepper. Cook, stirring occasionally, until they soften and the onion becomes translucent, about 5 minutes.

Stir in the potatoes and the corn and toss to coat with the onion mixture. Season well with salt—and I mean well, like a good, heaping palmful; the potatoes need the salt. I promise it won't be too salty.

Pour in the stock and bring to a boil, then reduce to a simmer, partially cover, and cook, stirring occasionally, until the potatoes are tender, 15 to 20 minutes.

Pour in the cream and allow it to simmer (not boil) for a minute or so. Stir in the crabmeat, remove the pot from the heat, and leave it covered for about 5 minutes. It will still be hot when it's time to serve.

To serve: Ladle into bowls and garnish with some thinly sliced scallions, basil, and/or roughly chopped corn nuts. Taste and adjust seasonings accordingly with salt and a good few turns of freshly ground black pepper.

Creamy Roasted Squash Soup *with* Gnocchi Croutons *and* Pancetta

SERVES
4 to 6

TIME
1 hour

INGREDIENTS

2 Honeynut squash (about 2 pounds/910 g), halved lengthwise with seeds discarded
3 medium shallots, halved lengthwise with skin kept on
¼ cup (60 ml), plus 2 tablespoons extra-virgin olive oil
Kosher salt and freshly ground black pepper
2 ounces (55 g) pancetta
6 cups (1.4 L) chicken stock, plus more as needed
4 cloves garlic, finely chopped
½ teaspoon red pepper flakes
2 tablespoons finely chopped fresh sage
½ cup (120 ml) heavy cream
6 ounces (170 g) shelf-stable gnocchi
Grated Parmesan (optional), for serving

This is a celebration soup if ever there was one. It's indulgent, over the top, and absolutely worth it. Toasted gnocchi for croutons? Come on! It would also be a lovely, sipping starter to add to the Thanksgiving menu. If you do, I'd serve it in a demitasse cup as she is a rich dish, and you'll only need a small serving with all that food ahead of you. Roasting the squash and the shallots brings out their sweetness and if you'd like to make this dish vegetarian, simply leave out the pancetta and use vegetable stock in lieu of chicken. This dish is fancy enough for a dinner party, served with a big, bright green salad and chocolate bars and citrus for dessert.

METHOD

Preheat the oven to 425°F (220°C).

On a sheet pan, drizzle the squash and shallots with ¼ cup (60 ml) olive oil. Season with salt and pepper. Roast the squash cut side up alongside the shallots until very tender, 30 to 35 minutes.

Meanwhile, line a plate with paper towels and have near the stove. Add the pancetta to a cold 12-inch (30 cm) sauté pan or Dutch oven. Cook over medium-low heat until crispy and golden, 5 to 7 minutes. With a slotted spoon, transfer to the paper towels.

When the squash and shallots are cool enough to touch, scrape out the flesh and slip the shallots from their skins. Transfer to a blender and add 2 cups (480 ml) of the chicken stock and pulse together until everything is smooth and puree-like.

In a large Dutch oven, heat the remaining 2 tablespoons of olive oil over medium heat. Add the garlic, pepper flakes, and sage and cook until fragrant, about 30 seconds. Add the squash mixture to the pot along with the remaining 4 cups (946 ml) stock and stir to combine. Pour in the cream and cook, stirring frequently until it just begins to thicken, about 5 minutes. Add more broth if you want it a bit looser.

Meanwhile, in a separate nonstick or cast-iron skillet, heat 2 tablespoons of olive oil over medium heat. Add the gnocchi in one layer and cook, flipping once, until golden and crispy, about 4 minutes total. Take off the heat.

Taste the soup and season with salt and pepper. Ladle into bowls and top each with some of the gnocchi and scatter with pancetta and grated Parmesan if you like.

Udon Soup *with* Shiitakes, Cabbage, *and an* Egg Yolk

SERVES
4

TIME
30 minutes

INGREDIENTS

3 tablespoons neutral oil, such as grapeseed or vegetable, plus more as needed
8 ounces (225 g) shiitake mushrooms, stems discarded, caps torn into bite-size pieces
Kosher salt
½ medium white onion, finely chopped
2 celery stalks, thinly sliced
5 cloves garlic, roughly chopped
2 Thai bird's eye chiles, thinly sliced
1 tablespoon grated fresh ginger
6 cups (1.4 L) vegetable broth—low sodium if store bought
2 tablespoons soy sauce
4 cups (280 g) thinly sliced napa cabbage
1 package (10 ounces/280 g) dried udon
4 egg yolks

for serving:
Toasted sesame seeds
Thinly sliced scallions
Roughly chopped celery leaves

I'm a sucker for a noodle soup of any kind and this vegetarian one perfectly fits the bill and comes together in no time to boot. Don't rush the browning process with the mushrooms as they offer great depth to the broth, and the egg yolk is not only pretty to look at but also adds a beautifully viscosity to the soup. Savoy cabbage can be subbed for the napa variety as could baby bok choy. Also, please don't skimp on toppings: Any soup worth its spoon relies on them for another great layer of flavor and texture.

METHOD

In a large Dutch oven, heat the oil over medium heat. Add the mushrooms and cook, stirring occasionally, until deeply brown, 7 to 8 minutes. Season with salt.

Stir in the onion, celery, garlic, and chiles and cook until they begin to soften, 3 to 5 minutes, adding a bit more oil if the pan is looking dry. Stir in the ginger and cook for 30 seconds more. Season with salt.

Add the broth and the soy sauce and bring to a simmer. Keep simmering so all the flavors get to know each other a bit better, 20 minutes or so. Add the cabbage and cook until it begins to soften, about 3 minutes. Taste and adjust the broth with more salt as needed.

Meanwhile, cook the udon noodles according to the package directions, drain, and evenly divide the udon noodles among four bowls.

Ladle the soup over top and gently place an egg yolk on top of each portion. Top with some of the sesame seeds, scallions, and celery leaves.

PASTA POTS & PIZZA PIES

Spicy Crab Pasta *with* Toasted Lemon Crumbs

SERVES
4

TIME
35 minutes

INGREDIENTS
for the pasta:
Kosher salt
12 ounces (340 g) bucatini
3 large shallots, peeled and roughly chopped
4 cloves garlic, peeled but whole
2 fresh cayenne or Fresno chiles, or 1 teaspoon red pepper flakes
¼ cup (60 ml) extra-virgin olive oil
1 cup (240 ml) dry white wine
2 cups (480 ml) tomato passata

for the bread crumbs:
1 tablespoon extra-virgin olive oil
⅓ cup (25 g) panko bread crumbs
1 teaspoon grated lemon zest
Flaky salt

to finish:
¾ to 1 pound (340 to 455 g) lump crabmeat
4 tablespoons (60 g) butter
½ cup (25 g) roughly chopped fresh Italian parsley, basil, or mint, or combination of all three

I normally wouldn't ask you to take out your food processor to make what is essentially a soffritto, but I want the garlic, shallots, and chiles to essentially melt into the sauce, and pulsing it a few times will help turn it into more of a paste. You can of course chop everything very finely by hand, but using this tool will get you there faster. The reason behind this is that I really want the beautiful lumps of crab to shine and be the texture you're getting within your twirly bites of glossy sauce. I make this request because I want what's best for you! I hope you'll heed my plea.

METHOD

Make the pasta: Bring a large pot of well-salted water to a boil. Add pasta and cook to al dente according to the package directions. Reserving 1 cup (240 ml) of the pasta cooking water, drain the pasta.

In a mini-prep or small food processor, pulse the shallots, garlic, and chiles until they form a paste.

In a 12-inch (30 cm) skillet, heat the olive oil over medium heat until it shimmers. Add the shallot/chile paste to the pan and season with salt. Cook, stirring frequently, until it begins to soften and turn slightly golden, 5 to 7 minutes.

Add the white wine and cook until it reduces by half, 1 to 2 minutes more. Stir in the passata and bring to a very gentle simmer over low heat. Cook, stirring occasionally, for 10 to 15 minutes, so the flavors can get to know one another. Taste and season with salt as needed.

Meanwhile, make the bread crumbs: In a 12-inch (30 cm) skillet, heat the oil over medium-low heat. Add the panko and toast, stirring frequently, until golden, 2 to 4 minutes. Transfer the crumbs to a small bowl and toss together with the lemon zest and season with flaky salt.

To finish: When you're ready to serve, add the drained pasta, crab, and butter to the sauce in the skillet and toss together gently, until the pasta is glossy with sauce, but the crab retains much of its structure. Add a few tablespoons of the pasta water if needed to loosen up the sauce.

Transfer to a large bowl or four pasta bowls and top with some of the bread crumbs and the chopped herbs. Pass the remaining bread crumbs at the table, should you want to spoon more on top (and you will . . .).

Manhattan Clam Pasta

SERVES
4

TIME
20 minutes

INGREDIENTS

Kosher salt
12 ounces (340 g) linguine
2 tablespoons extra-virgin olive oil
2 tablespoons (30 g) unsalted butter
1 large shallot, finely chopped
4 cloves garlic, finely chopped
3 tablespoons tomato paste
2 tablespoons ‘nduja
3 pounds (1.4 kg) littleneck clams, scrubbed and soaked to rid grit
½ cup (120 ml) white wine
2 tablespoons finely chopped fresh Italian parsley
1 lemon, cut into wedges, for serving
Grated pecorino cheese (optional), for serving

As you may know, clams are one of my absolutely most favorite foods. This fun take on traditional vongole was created solely so I could have another way to eat more of them. This recipe uses a combination of tomato paste and smoky ‘nduja (a spicy spreadable sausage from Calabria) to give it its fiery color. Should you want to make it pescatarian, simply leave it out and up the tomato paste. I also suggested topping this with grated pecorino cheese. Since I'm already breaking the rules of a classic Italian dish and likely to be lambasted by purists, I say to hell with it, and go all in.

METHOD

Bring a large pot of well-salted water to a boil. Add the pasta and cook until al dente according to the package directions. Reserving 1 cup (240 ml) of the pasta cooking water, drain the pasta.

Meanwhile, heat a large Dutch oven over medium heat. Add the olive oil and the butter and once the butter melts, add the shallot and garlic and cook until softened, about 2 minutes. Add the tomato paste and the ‘nduja and toast the tomato paste until it turns a brick red, about 2 minutes more. Stir everything together until well combined.

Add the clams and pour in the white wine. Bring to a simmer, cover, and cook, shaking the pan occasionally, until the clams begin to pop open, 7 to 9 minutes total. Discard any that do not.

Add the pasta to the sauce with a bit of the pasta water and toss until everything is well combined and the pasta is glossy with sauce, adding more pasta water as needed.

Plate in bowls and garnish with the Italian parsley and a good squeeze of lemon juice. Pass the grated cheese at the table, if desired.

The Days After Christmas

Everyone, myself included, is bustling in the days leading up to the holidays and while they genuinely thrill me, it's Boxing Day and the days between Christmas and New Years that bring me the most joy. There are leftovers to eat, many people to share them with, and the pressure of it actually being Christmas is miraculously gone. It is the laziest, most indulgent week in between the new year and the old. It is a putter about your house in pajamas, and a fumble around the kitchen in woolen socks for days on end sort of debauchery, wearing your coziest pants.

For the last five years, Chad and I have moved in with Helen and Dan for a good part of this week. It is true that there is less than a 10-minute walk between our homes, but it feels special to camp out with our chosen family. Champagne for breakfast is generally encouraged, paired with a (yesterday's) Christmas ham sandwich slathered with mustard on a potato roll and topped with cornichons. Alternatively, Helen kindly makes us bacon sarnies coupled with a strong mug of tea. Sometimes we are heathens and have both.

The afternoon usually starts with beer for the boys and bubbles for Helen and myself, with perhaps another sandwich or wedge of reheated lasagna (page 126) in the afternoon. This party doesn't move locations too often from the imprint of the cozy leather couch, but Helen does generally force us on some sort of nature walk with Sugo the dog, which we begrudgingly agree to and then always absolutely enjoy. We will never learn and she often knows best. And then it's back home to the couch for a movie, where afternoons turn quickly into evenings and you've realized you've done it again.

When we eventually move home, there have been days when Chad and I allow ourselves to stay in bed until questionably late in the morning. Those who know me, know that this is very unlike me; I am an up-at-7:30 a.m. gal, but somehow, I am able to allow myself to go with the flow for this one week each year. Going back and forth between sweatpants to pajamas by now has become a very regular "ready to wear" look. Lean in.

On a few of these mornings we wake up craving something else. A number of dishes come to mind such as smash burgers, hand-pulled noodles with lamb and spicy Sichuan chili oil, or dim sum to name just a few. On that day we will pile into the car and make the forty-minute drive to Albany to satiate our hankerings. We will also stop by the Asian market to pick up ingredients for New Year's Eve—Chad has made Peking duck for as long as I can remember—and I will go into a shopping frenzy piling a variety of noodles, frozen dumplings, and unusual condiments for future use. We return well-stocked and well-fed.

New Year's Eve always comes more quickly than we'd like—it's so nice to have those days of absolute nothingness—but it does give us the occasion to all reconvene for more festivities. Our last gathering included not only the duck, but Asian wings, sesame noodles, and soup dumplings, and a total of eleven people. I sabered a bottle of champagne and stayed up till 4 a.m. It was a thrill.

The ham returns for its final debut as we close out the week as it is custom that I make soup for New Year's Day with the bone and beans (page 98). Bleary-eyed, we make our way next door to Kelly's where she has bagels, lox, and all the trimmings to celebrate some more, and when we need something of more sustenance, I'll begin warming the soup for guests and scouring for bowls to ladle it into. It always does the trick.

Depending on fatigue, we'll head home early in the evening. As the first day of the new year closes, my cup feels very full and I consider all of our lounging and indulging without guilt to be a good omen for the near new year ahead. I, of course, am already plotting the next round of shenanigans.

Pressing cider with Sophie while drinking the batch she made with Harry the year before.

Fregola "Risotto" with Currants, Pine Nuts, and Fried Capers **(136)**

A Christmas Lasagna

SERVES
8 to 10

TIME
4 hours

This lasagna is a labor of love, but so worth the lift. Chad is usually the one in charge of making this dish for the holidays, but I have taken the reins as of late. This sauce is made in a Bolognese-type fashion but uses a bit more tomatoes than the traditional sauce calls for. In the past, we've made fresh pasta for this dish, and if you feel like going the extra mile, please do! I call for dried pasta here for ease and accessibility. I also incorporate crème fraîche into my cheese mixture for extra creaminess. You can make this dish a few days in advance or even get ahead by making the sauce solo—then all you need to do is assemble. As mentioned, we make this each year for Christmas, but this lasagna is so good, it shouldn't be relegated to once a year. Make it this weekend for friends.

INGREDIENTS

for the sauce:

- 1 medium onion, roughly chopped
- 1 medium carrot, roughly chopped
- 1 celery stalk, roughly chopped
- 2 ounces (55 g) pancetta, chopped
- 2 tablespoons extra-virgin olive oil
- 2 tablespoons (30 g) butter
- 1 tablespoon fresh sage (optional)
- Kosher salt
- 1 pound (455 g) ground pork
- 1 pound (455 g) ground beef
- ¼ cup (66 g) tomato paste
- 1 cup (240 ml) dry white wine
- 1 cup (240 ml) whole milk
- ¼ teaspoon freshly grated nutmeg
- 2 cups (480 ml) beef or chicken stock (I use Better Than Bouillon to make my stock)
- 1 can (28 ounces/794 g) crushed tomatoes

for the lasagna:

- 1 pound (455 g) fresh mozzarella cheese
- 1 cup (245 g) whole-milk ricotta
- 8 ounces (225 g) crème fraîche
- ⅓ cup (30 g) grated pecorino cheese, plus 2 tablespoons, for topping
- Kosher salt and freshly ground black pepper
- A few scrapes of freshly grated nutmeg
- 1 pound (455 g) dried lasagna noodles
- Olive oil, for drizzling

METHOD

Make the sauce: In a food processor, pulse together the onion, carrot, celery, and pancetta, until finely chopped.

In a large Dutch oven, heat the olive oil and melt the butter over medium heat. Add the chopped vegetable/pancetta mixture and cook until translucent, 5 to 6 minutes. Add the sage (if using) and cook for 1 minute more. Season with salt. Add the pork and beef, breaking the meat up with the back of a spoon and cook until it is no longer pink, 6 to 7 minutes.

Add the tomato paste and toast for a minute or two, and then stir to incorporate with the meat. Season with salt. Add the white wine and cook until it evaporates, 7 to 10 minutes.

Add the milk and the nutmeg and cook until it evaporates, 7 to 10 minutes more.

Add the stock and let it reduce by half, about 10 minutes more. Add the tomatoes and stir everything together. Reduce the heat to low and simmer until the meat is completely tender and the color of the sauce is rich and ruddy, 1½ to 2 hours, adding small splashes of broth or water, as needed, to ensure the sauce doesn't dry out. Taste and adjust seasonings with more salt if needed.

Preheat the oven to 400°F (200°C).

Assemble the lasagna: Finely grate three-quarters of the mozzarella. Tear the rest and set aside to top the lasagna with.

In a bowl, stir together the grated mozzarella, ricotta, crème fraîche, and ⅓ cup (30 g) of the pecorino and season with a bit of salt (the pecorino is already salty), black pepper, and the nutmeg. Set aside.

In a large pot of well-salted boiling water, boil the lasagna noodles for 3 minutes. Transfer to a sheet pan and drizzle with olive oil to prevent them from sticking.

In an 11 by 13-inch (28 by 33 cm) baking dish, ladle in some of the sauce and spread to cover the bottom of the dish. Top with a layer of the noodles, followed by more sauce and one-third of the cheese mixture. Repeat with remaining noodles, sauce, and cheese. The final layer should be sauce. Top with the reserved torn mozzarella and the remaining 2 tablespoons pecorino. Tent with foil (this will help the cheese from sticking to the top) and transfer to the oven.

Bake until everything is warmed through and the cheese is beginning to melt, 20 to 25 minutes. Uncover and cook until the edges of the lasagna become crispy and golden and the cheese does too, 20 to 25 more minutes. Allow to cool slightly for 10 to 15 minutes, slice, and serve.

Tuna Noodle *with* String Beans *and* Sesame

SERVES
2 generously

TIME
20 minutes

INGREDIENTS
for the dressing:

¼ cup (60 ml) tahini, such as Seed + Mill
2 tablespoons soy sauce
2 tablespoons fresh lime juice (from 1 lime)
1 teaspoon honey
1 teaspoon grated fresh ginger
1 tablespoon of your favorite chili crisp
½ teaspoon toasted sesame oil
1 tablespoon warm water, plus more as needed
Kosher salt

for the noodles and tuna:

4 ounces (115 g) fresh wheat noodles, such as ramen or udon
8 ounces (225 g) string beans, snap peas, or other snappy vegetable, thinly sliced on the bias
Toasted sesame oil, for drizzling
¼ cup (35 g) sesame seeds
2 tuna steaks (6 ounces/170 g each), about 1½ inches (4 cm) thick
1 tablespoon canola oil
Flaky salt
2 scallions, thinly sliced on the bias, dark-green parts kept separate
¼ cup (12 g) loosely packed, roughly chopped herbs, such as mint, cilantro, and basil
1 teaspoon toasted sesame seeds (optional), for garnish

This is decidedly an early aughts tuna preparation, which I can remember being on many menus at the various restaurants I worked at in my twenties. I'm thrilled to bring it back into fashion. This dish is sophisticated and also dead simple, making it as good for a weeknight as it is if you're celebrating something special. I like using a combination of both black and white sesame seeds for presentation's sake, but if only white ones are within reach, it will still look striking. The tuna sits atop a tangle of noodles and green beans, which are tossed in a sesame dressing, hopefully introducing this new dish into the current decade.

METHOD

Make the dressing: In a medium bowl, whisk together the tahini, soy sauce, lime juice, honey, ginger, chili crisp, sesame oil, and warm water. If needed, add a bit more water to loosen up the sauce. Season with kosher salt, taste, and adjust seasonings accordingly.

Cook the noodles: Bring a large pot of water to a boil, add the noodles and the string beans, and cook according to the package directions—this should be 2 to 3 minutes for fresh noodles. Drain and rinse under cool running water and drizzle with a bit of sesame oil to prevent the noodles from sticking together.

Cook the tuna: Pour the sesame seeds onto a dinner plate. Press the tuna steaks into the sesame seeds firmly on both sides, so they evenly coat the fish.

Heat a medium nonstick skillet over medium-high heat. Add the canola oil and when it shimmers add the tuna. Sear the tuna for 1 to 1½ minutes on each side for medium-rare. Transfer to a cutting board, sprinkle with flaky salt, and cut into ¼ inch slices.

Transfer the noodles and string beans to a large bowl. Add the scallion whites and light-green parts and half the herbs and toss gently with the dressing.

Divide the noodles between two large bowls and top each with the seared tuna, reserved scallion greens, remaining herbs, and toasted sesame seeds (if using).

Brothy Clams *with* Small Pasta *and* Summer Corn

SERVES
4

TIME
30 minutes

INGREDIENTS

Kosher salt

8 ounces (225 g) dried cappelletti or other small pasta such as orecchiette

2 tablespoons extra-virgin olive oil, plus more as needed

4 ounces (115 g) pancetta

4 scallions, finely chopped, dark-green parts kept separate

4 cloves garlic, thinly sliced

1 medium jalapeño, finely chopped

3 medium ears corn, kernels removed

½ cup (120 ml) white wine

2 dozen littleneck or cherrystone clams, soaked and scrubbed

2 tablespoons (30 g) unsalted butter

Grated zest and juice of 1 large lemon

Freshly ground black pepper

2 tablespoons roughly chopped fresh Italian parsley

This pasta is one for late summer when corn is at its sweetest here on the East Coast. Clams, too, call to me year-round, but especially when I'm by the ocean, where I happen to be in Nova Scotia from July to September. This dish is decidedly more on the soupier end of pasta and should be eaten in bowls and maybe even with a spoon? If you can't find dried cappelletti, use orecchiette or even ditalini. Crusty bread for dipping is always a good idea, as is eating outside.

METHOD

Bring a large pot of well-salted water to a boil. Add the pasta and cook to 2 to 3 minutes shy of al dente. Reserving 1 cup (240 ml) of the cooking water (you may need it, you may not, but better safe than sorry), drain the pasta.

Meanwhile, line a plate with paper towels and have near the stove. In a large Dutch oven or soup pot, heat the olive oil over medium heat. Add the pancetta and cook until golden and crispy, 6 to 7 minutes. Transfer with a slotted spoon to the paper towels.

Add the scallion whites and light-green parts, the garlic, jalapeño, and corn to the pot and stir to coat in the pancetta oil, adding a bit more olive oil if needed. Cook until the scallions and garlic are softened and the corn begins to turn golden in spots, 5 to 6 minutes.

Stir in the white wine and the clams, bring to a simmer and cover. At around the 6-minute mark, peek under the lid to see if the clams have started popping open, remove those that have to a bowl and remove them from their shells, keeping them with their juices. Check in another minute or so to remove the rest and repeat.

Reduce the heat to low, stir in the butter along with the reserved clams and the pasta, and cook until the butter has melted and the pasta is glossy with sauce. It should be more brothy than a normal pasta dish; if needed add a few tablespoons of the reserved pasta water.

Add the lemon zest, lemon juice, and a few good turns of black pepper. Stir again, taste, and adjust with more salt and pepper as needed. Scatter with the scallion greens and parsley. Ladle into bowls.

A Note: You'll see the photograph has dam shells in it. I did this for purely aesthetic reasons! You can choose whether or not to remove all the dams from their shells—half and half is also a good option.

Crispy Lamb Flatbreads *with* Feta *and* Honey

SERVES
4

TIME
20 minutes if using store-bought pitas; 3½ hours if making homemade

INGREDIENTS

1 pound (455 g) ground lamb
1 tablespoon harissa
1 teaspoon ground cardamom
1 teaspoon ground cumin
1 teaspoon kosher salt
½ teaspoon ground cinnamon
3 scallions, thinly sliced
2 teaspoons preserved lemon paste, or 1 tablespoon fresh lemon juice
Dough for 4 large Homemade Flatbreads (page 226) or 4 (12-inch/30 cm) store-bought round pitas
2½ ounces (70 g) crumbled feta cheese
Olive oil, for brushing
Toasted sesame seeds
Roughly chopped fresh mint and cilantro, for serving
Hot honey, for serving

I love ground lamb, and this recipe is the perfect vehicle for enjoying it. I use classic Middle Eastern flavors, such as harissa paste and cumin and a bit of cinnamon, which play really well with its savoriness. The preserved lemon helps cut the fat, but if regular lemon is what you've got, use it instead. I highly recommend making your own flatbread for this to make it extra special and celebratory. That said, if you're short on time, use store-bought pitas, but I'd be lying if I said you wouldn't be missing out! This recipe feeds four as a main course, but if you cut the flatbreads in half or in quarters, they would also be a great pre-dinner snack alongside some creamy dips and olives.

METHOD

Preheat the oven to 450°F (230°C). Line a large sheet pan with parchment paper.

In a large bowl, combine the lamb, harissa, cardamom, cumin, kosher salt, cinnamon, scallions, and the preserved lemon paste or lemon juice. Stir everything together until it is well combined.

Working two at a time, roll out the flatbreads until they are ¼ inch (6 mm) thick. These can be whatever shape you like, I tend to go round as opposed to long. Transfer to the baking sheet. If you're using store-bought pitas you should skip this step!

Using half of the lamb mixture, take a spatula and spread it evenly onto the rolled-out doughs, leaving about ¼ inch (6 mm) around the edges. Top with some of the feta cheese.

Brush the edges of the dough with a bit of olive oil and give the flatbread a few shakes of sesame seeds so they stick.

Bake until golden brown, 8 to 10 minutes. Top with herbs and drizzle with hot honey. Repeat with the remaining flatbreads.

Early Summer Pasta *with* Torn Noodles, Mascarpone, *and* Hazelnuts

SERVES
4

TIME
25 minutes

INGREDIENTS

Kosher salt

12 ounces (340 g) lasagna noodles broken into roughly 2-inch (5 cm) pieces

¼ cup (35 g) hazelnuts (no need to remove their skins)

¼ cup (60 ml) extra-virgin olive oil

1½ pounds (680 g) baby zucchini, thinly sliced into rounds

1 pint (300 g) Sungold tomatoes or other small varietal tomato

4 cloves garlic, finely chopped

½ teaspoon red pepper flakes

1½ teaspoons dried mint

⅓ cup (75 g) mascarpone cheese

2 tablespoons grated pecorino cheese, plus more for serving

¼ cup (13 g) roughly chopped fresh mint

¼ cup (11 g) finely chopped chives, with their blossoms if available

Technically you don't have to wait until early summer to make this pasta as you can find the ingredients pretty much year-round in the grocery store. That said, it does really taste even better with first-of-the-season produce. I love using lasagna noodles for other dishes other than traditional lasagna, which work well here. It's easy and quick and perfect for a weeknight, but pretty enough for a pasta party should you throw one.

METHOD

Bring a large pot of well-salted water to a boil. Add the pasta and cook to al dente, 8 to 10 minutes. Reserving 1 cup (240 ml) of pasta water, drain the pasta.

Meanwhile, heat a 12-inch (30 cm) sauté pan over medium heat. Add the hazelnuts and toast, stirring frequently so they don't burn, 3 to 4 minutes. Transfer to a plate and when cool enough to touch, roughly chop, and set aside.

Wipe out the pan and heat the olive oil over medium heat. Add the zucchini, season with salt, and cook until they begin to soften and turn slightly golden, 3 to 4 minutes. Stir in the Sungolds and season again with salt. Cook until the tomatoes begin to burst and become jammy, 5 to 7 minutes more. Add the garlic, pepper flakes, and dried mint and cook until the garlic is fragrant, about 1 minute more.

Reduce the heat to medium-low and stir in the mascarpone, pecorino, and ⅓ cup (75 ml) pasta water and stir everything together until silky. Cook for 1 minute more to thicken the sauce slightly. Add the pasta and a bit more pasta water, as needed, and stir until everything is glossy with sauce.

Top with the fresh mint, chives, and the hazelnuts and serve straight from the pan. (Alternatively, serve on a platter or in bowls and then top with the herbs and nuts.) Pass more pecorino at the table.

Fregola "Risotto" *with* Currants, Pine Nuts, *and* Fried Capers

SERVES
4

TIME
30 minutes

INGREDIENTS
- 2 tablespoons dried currants
- 2 tablespoons sherry vinegar
- 2 tablespoons pine nuts
- 8 cups (2 L) vegetable, chicken, or beef stock
- 2 tablespoons extra-virgin olive oil, plus more as needed
- 2 tablespoons capers, drained and patted dry if in brine
- 1 large shallot, finely chopped
- 12 ounces (340 g) fregola
- ½ cup (120 ml) dry vermouth or white wine
- ¼ cup (25 g) grated pecorino cheese, plus more for serving
- 3 tablespoons (45 g) unsalted butter
- 2 tablespoons finely chopped fresh Italian parsley
- Freshly ground black pepper

In lieu of Arborio rice, I've opted to cook fregola—a small, hard durum wheat flour pasta hailing from Sardinia—in the same method one would a traditional risotto. Because fregola is dried and then toasted, it imparts a wonderfully nutty flavor when cooked and is more forgiving/less fussy. Soaking currants in a bit of vinegar not only plumps them up a bit, but adds nice brightness, and topping your bowls with crispy capers for a crunchy, salty bit and toasted pine nuts for texture makes for a perfect bite. You could serve this on its own with a salad of bitter greens—I have. It would also pair nicely as a side to braised meat or roast chicken. When developing this, I initially put it off because flavor profile–wise I didn't think it was going to be a "Chad" dish and he's my first tester. But, as soon as he had one bite, he said "You did it again!" I'm glad I did.

METHOD

In a small bowl, combine the currants and vinegar. Set aside.

Heat a large Dutch oven or skillet over medium heat. Add the pine nuts and toast, stirring frequently, until golden, 3 to 5 minutes. Transfer to a small bowl and set aside.

Meanwhile, in a large saucepan, bring the chicken stock to a simmer.

Line a plate with paper towels and have near the stove. In the same pan you used to toast the pine nuts, heat the olive oil until it shimmers. Add the capers and toast until crispy, 2 to 3 minutes. With a slotted spoon, transfer to the paper towels.

Add the shallot to the pan and cook until soft and translucent, 3 to 4 minutes. Add the fregola to the pan and stir to coat in the oil. Add the vermouth to deglaze pan and then cook until the liquid is reduced by half, about 2 minutes.

Stir in 1 cup (240 ml) of stock. Cook, stirring constantly until the pasta has absorbed most of the stock. Continue stirring and adding ladlesful of stock until the pasta is almost tender, 15 to 20 minutes.

Remove the skillet from the heat and add the currants in their vinegar, the pecorino, and butter and toss until the butter has melted.

Ladle into bowls and top each portion with some of the capers, pine nuts, and the parsley. Pass a pepper mill and more pecorino at the table.

Pizza Dough

MAKES
enough for four 10-inch (25 cm) pizzas

TIME
3½ hours (indudes rising time)

INGREDIENTS

1 (7 g) envelope instant yeast (2¼ teaspoons)
2 cups (480 ml) warm water
5 cups (625 g) all-purpose flour
1 tablespoon kosher salt
Olive oil

There is no better pizza dough recipe than the recipe from Chris Bianco of Pizzeria Bianco in Phoenix, Arizona. He also makes the best canned tomatoes . . . This recipe is adapted from his because I'm not in a position to mess with a good thing and I am very much of the "if it ain't broke, don't fix it" mindset. Chad used to be the pizzaiolo in the house, but ever since I started making the dough, his position has been replaced. We have a wood-fired pizza oven in Nova Scotia and a lot of house guests, which means I make a lot of pizza. If you don't have a wood-fired oven, invest in a pizza stone and heat your kitchen oven with the stone at 500°F (260°C) until it's very, very hot.

METHOD

In a large bowl, whisk together the yeast and the water—little bubbles should form, which will show you that the yeast is activated.

Mix in 3 cups (375 g) of the flour gradually until it is hydrated. I usually use a large wooden spoon for this bit and then switch over to my hands. Gradually add in the remaining 2 cups (250 g) flour, making sure it is well incorporated into the dough. Add the salt and mix until it is worked in throughout.

Transfer the dough to a floured surface and knead for 5 to 7 minutes until it is extremely tacky and sticky and work it into a ball. Oil a large bowl and transfer the dough, rolling it around to make sure all sides are slick with oil. Cover with plastic wrap and let it rise until doubled in size, about 2 hours.

With a pastry scraper or sharp knife, cut the dough into 4 equal portions. Shape them into balls and dust with flour. Cover and let them rise until they have doubled in size, about 1 hour more.

Use immediately or put in the fridge for up to 3 days or freeze for up to 6 months.

A Few Notes on Making Pizzas

1. Invest in a pizza stone and put it in the oven for at least 1 hour before cooking—you'll need to get it very hot for your pizzas to get crispy. I've written these recipes for the kitchen oven for ease, but please feel free to make them in your pizza oven, such as a Gozney or an Ooni, should you have one.

2. Buy a pizza wheel for cutting your pies. It makes life easier.

3. Have your pizza toppings all ready to go before you shape the dough. You'll need to work quickly once the dough is on the pizza stone.

4. Less is more when it comes to the base of your pies. You don't want to make your pizzas too wet on the bottom. Not only will they not get crisp, but the pizzas become difficult to maneuver.

5. Pizza is similar to pasta in terms of creating fun flavor profiles. Play around! I've included some of my favorites, but you should feel free to riff with your favorite ingredients. Other combinations I love are:

   Clams + Lemon + Fresh Chiles + Pecorino
   Taleggio + Radicchio + Pistachios
   Zucchini + Corn + Sungolds
   Fennel + Prosciutto + Mushroom
   Honeynut Squash + Mascarpone + Sage

6. On that note, throw many pizza parties! We do it every summer in Nova Scotia and once we did it at our friend Emma and Dom's for thirty people in December. Everyone hangs out in the kitchen or by the oven and has fun coming up with their own signature pie. The only other things you'll need are beer and wine.

Pizza *with* Dates, Blue Cheese, *and* Shallots

MAKES
one 10-inch (25 cm) pizza

TIME
15 minutes

INGREDIENTS
1 ball Pizza Dough (page 138)
Semolina flour, for dusting
4 ounces (115 g) Roquefort or other good-quality blue cheese, crumbled
5 pitted dates, torn
1 shallot, thinly sliced into rings
2 tablespoons extra-virgin olive oil
Flaky salt, for finishing

METHOD

About 1 hour before you're ready to make the pizza, place a pizza stone in the oven and preheat it as high as it will go. You want the stone as hot as possible.

Have your pizza toppings ready to go before you shape the dough as you'll need to work quickly.

Remove the pizza stone from the oven and dust with a bit of semolina flour. Shape the pizza dough into a 10-inch (25 cm) round and transfer to the pizza stone.

Top the pizza evenly with the blue cheese, dates, and shallot and drizzle with the olive oil.

Place in the oven and bake until the blue cheese begins to bubble and the edges are slightly crispy, 8 to 10 minutes.

Transfer the pizza carefully to a cutting board. Finish with a few pinches of flaky salt. Slice and serve.

Pizza *with* Potato, 'Nduja, *and* Mozzarella

MAKES
one 10-inch (25 cm) pizza

TIME
15 minutes

INGREDIENTS
1 ball Pizza Dough (page 138)
Semolina flour, for dusting
3 ounces (85 g) fresh mozzarella cheese, torn
1 small waxy potato, very thinly sliced (use a mandoline if you're comfortable)
Kosher salt
2½ ounces (70 g) 'nduja
Olive oil, for drizzling
Flaky salt, for finishing

METHOD

About 1 hour before you're ready to make the pizza, place a pizza stone in the oven and preheat it as high as it will go. You want the stone as hot as possible.

Have your pizza toppings ready to go before you shape the dough as you'll need to work quickly.

Remove the pizza stone from the oven and dust with a bit of semolina flour. Shape the pizza dough into a 10-inch (25 cm) round and transfer to the pizza stone.

Top the pizza evenly with the torn mozzarella and then top with the potatoes, trying not to overlap them too much. Season with kosher salt. Dot the pizza with the 'nduja and drizzle with a bit of olive oil.

Place in the oven and bake until the cheese bubbles and the 'nduja melts, 8 to 10 minutes.

Transfer the pizza carefully to a cutting board. Finish with a few pinches of flaky salt. Slice and serve.

Pizza *with* Soppressata *and* Pickled Peppers

MAKES
one 10-inch (25 cm) pizza

TIME
15 minutes

INGREDIENTS

1 ball Pizza Dough (page 138)
Semolina flour, for dusting
2 to 3 tablespoons passata
A few pinches of dried oregano
3 ounces (85 g) fresh mozzarella cheese, torn
1 ounce (28 g) thinly sliced soppressata
Olive oil, for drizzling
Flaky salt, for finishing
Pickled banana peppers, for serving

METHOD

About 1 hour before you're ready to make the pizza, place a pizza stone in the oven and preheat it as high as it will go. You want the stone as hot as possible.

Have your pizza toppings ready to go before you shape the dough as you'll need to work quickly.

Remove the pizza stone from the oven and dust with semolina flour. Shape the pizza dough into a 10-inch (25 cm) round and transfer to the pizza stone.

Spread the passata evenly around the pizza dough and add a few good pinches of dried oregano. Top evenly with the mozzarella followed by the soppressata and drizzle with some olive oil.

Place in the oven and bake until the cheese begins to bubble and the soppressata begins to get crispy, 8 to 10 minutes.

Transfer the pizza carefully to a cutting board. Finish with a few pinches of flaky salt. Slice and serve with the pickled banana peppers alongside.

Pizza *with* Lobster, Corn, *and* Jalapeño

MAKES
one 10-inch (25 cm) pizza

TIME
15 minutes

INGREDIENTS

1 ball Pizza Dough (page 138)
Semolina flour, for dusting
3 ounces (85 g) fresh mozzarella cheese, torn
2 tablespoons corn kernels
1 jalapeño, thinly sliced (seeded if you're concerned about spiciness)
1 tin (3 ounces/85 g) lobster meat, drained
Kosher salt
Olive oil, for drizzling
Flaky salt, for finishing

METHOD

About 1 hour before you're ready to make the pizza, place a pizza stone in the oven and preheat it as high as it will go. You want the stone as hot as possible.

Have your pizza toppings ready to go before you shape the dough as you'll need to work quickly.

Remove the pizza stone from the oven and dust with semolina flour. Shape the pizza dough into a 10-inch (25 cm) round and transfer to the pizza stone.

Top the pizza evenly with the mozzarella and scatter the corn and jalapeño on top, followed by the lobster meat. Season with kosher salt and drizzle with a bit of the olive oil.

Place in the oven and bake until the cheese begins to bubble and the jalapeño is slightly golden, 8 to 10 minutes.

Transfer the pizza carefully to a cutting board. Finish with a few pinches of flaky salt. Slice and serve.

Pizza *with* Ricotta, Caramelized Onion, *and* Hot Honey

MAKES
one 10-inch (25 cm) pizza

TIME
15 minutes

INGREDIENTS

1 ball Pizza Dough (page 138)
Semolina flour, for dusting
2 to 3 tablespoons ricotta
¼ cup (60 ml) Caramelized Onions (page 231)
Kosher salt
½ teaspoon red pepper flakes (optional)
Hot honey, for serving
Flaky salt, for finishing

METHOD

About 1 hour before you're ready to make the pizza, place a pizza stone in the oven and preheat it as high as it will go. You want the stone as hot as possible.

Have your pizza toppings ready to go before you shape the dough as you'll need to work quickly.

Remove the pizza stone from the oven and dust with a bit of semolina flour. Shape the pizza dough into a 10-inch (25 cm) round and transfer to the pizza stone.

Spread the ricotta evenly over the pizza leaving a ½-inch (12 mm) border. Dot with the caramelized onions and season with salt and the pepper flakes (if using).

Place in the oven and bake until the cheese begins to bubble, 8 to 10 minutes.

Transfer the pizza carefully to a cutting board and drizzle with hot honey. Finish with a few pinches of flaky salt. Slice and serve.

SHELLS & FISHES

Miso-Roasted Salmon *with* Soba Noodles in Broth

SERVES
4

TIME
30 minutes

INGREDIENTS
for the salmon and noodles:
1 tablespoon white miso
1 tablespoon mirin
½ teaspoon sesame oil
Splash of rice vinegar
1 pound (455 g) salmon
6 to 8 ounces (170 to 225 g) soba noodles

for the broth:
2 tablespoons neutral oil, such as canola
6 ounces (170 g) shiitake mushrooms, stems removed and pulled apart into bite-size pieces
3 scallions, thinly sliced, dark-green parts kept separate
1 tablespoon grated fresh ginger
2 cloves garlic, grated
1 Thai bird's eye chile, thinly sliced, or ½ to 1 teaspoon red pepper flakes
Kosher salt
4 cups (950 ml) vegetable broth, chicken stock, or water
8 ounces (225 g) baby bok choy, cut into 1-inch (2.5 cm) pieces

Sometimes a dish idea will come to me aesthetically first and I'll work backward trying to figure out how to make it happen. This is a very good example of that. I was craving something brothy and with salmon and noodles, but I didn't want it to be a soup per se. So! I decided instead to roast the salmon in a pleasantly sweet and salty marinade of miso, mirin, and sesame oil and then serve it in a bit of deeply flavorful broth on top of noodles. I made this for the first time on a cold January night for Chad and our nextdoor neighbor and friend Kelly and we all agreed the dish was cozy and comforting, but much more elegant than it had any right to be. I consider that a win. Make it any time of year you please.

METHOD

Preheat the oven to 400°F (200°C). Line a sheet pan with parchment paper or foil.

Prepare the salmon: In a small bowl, whisk together the miso, mirin, sesame oil, and vinegar. Taste and adjust seasonings as needed with more vinegar. Pour the mixture on top of the salmon and gently massage the marinade all over the fish. Let marinate while the oven comes to temperature.

Set the salmon on the sheet pan and roast until opaque, 10 to 12 minutes.

Meanwhile, cook the soba noodles according to the package directions. Drain and rinse with cold water to keep from sticking and evenly distribute among four bowls.

Build your broth: In a large Dutch oven or other heavy-bottomed pot, heat the oil over medium heat. Add the mushrooms and cook until they begin to brown around the edges, about 8 minutes. Add the scallion whites and light-green parts, ginger, garlic, and Thai chile and cook for 2 minutes more, until fragrant. Season with salt. Add the stock and bring to a simmer. Add the bok choy and cook to wilt. Taste and adjust the seasoning with salt as needed.

Spoon some of the broth over each bowl of noodles and flake the salmon on top, garnishing with the reserved scallion greens.

Rosy Roasted Cod *and* Potatoes *with* Punchy Sauce

SERVES
4 to 6

TIME
1 hour

INGREDIENTS
for the cod and potatoes:
- 5 tablespoons (75 ml) extra-virgin olive oil
- 2 tablespoons rose harissa paste, such as Belazu, or regular harissa paste (I like spicy, but use what spice level you prefer)
- 2 pounds (910 g) cod fillet, preferably wild-caught
- Kosher salt and freshly ground black pepper
- 2 pounds (910 g) Yukon Golds or others waxy potatoes, cut into rounds ⅛ inch (3 mm) thick
- 1 cup pitted Castelvetrano olives, halved lengthwise (about 4 ounces/115 g)

for the punchy sauce:
- 3 scallions, roughly chopped
- ½ cup (25 g) loosely packed mint leaves
- 1 cup (30 g) loosely packed cilantro, both leaves and tender stems
- 1 tablespoon preserved lemon paste or ¼ preserved lemon rind
- ¼ cup (60 ml) extra-virgin olive oil
- Kosher salt

January and February are my favorite months to host friends for the weekends in Hudson. Having someone to plan for, prep, and pamper gives me lightness in an otherwise bleak time of year. This recipe came about from one of those visits when Suzy, one of my oldest friends, came to stay. I asked her what she wanted for dinner and purposefully she said "fish!" Lucky for her, I had wild cod at the ready and we cooked and developed this recipe together. We lived together for four years, and I know she is very precise in her measurements. If you can find rose harissa paste, I highly recommend it for its floral notes, which plays nicely with the heat, but regular harissa paste will work fine, too. The crispy potatoes offer a lovely texture contrast with the silky cod, and the punchy sauce brings everything together with its brightness. Eat with dear friends.

METHOD

Preheat the oven to 400°F (200°C).

Cook the cod and potatoes: In a small bowl, whisk together 2 tablespoons of the olive oil with the harissa paste. Season the cod well with kosher salt and pepper and then with your hands or a spatula evenly coat the fish with the harissa mixture and set aside to marinate.

Meanwhile, in an 11 by 13-inch (28 by 33 cm) baking dish, toss the potatoes with the remaining 3 tablespoons of oil and season very well with salt and a few turns of freshly ground black pepper.

Roast the potatoes until they are tender and starting to crisp and turn golden, about 40 minutes, tossing the potatoes halfway through cooking time to ensure even cooking.

Remove the baking dish from the oven and stir the olives into the potato mixture and top with the cod. Return to the oven and roast until the fish is opaque and reaches 145°F (63°C), 15 to 18 minutes.

While the fish cooks, make the punchy sauce: In a food processor, combine the scallions, mint, cilantro, and preserved lemon paste or peel. Pulse together until very fine. Transfer to a medium bowl and stir in the olive oil and season with a bit of salt. Taste and adjust seasonings with salt to your preference. The preserved lemon is salty on its own, so go easy.

Spoon some of the sauce over the fish and serve directly in the baking dish. Pass the rest of the sauce at the table.

Pan-Seared Butter-Basted Sesame Scallops

SERVES
4

TIME
15 minutes

INGREDIENTS

16 large sea scallops, side muscle removed, patted very dry
1½ teaspoons fennel pollen (optional)
Kosher salt and freshly ground black pepper
¾ cup (115 g) sesame seeds
3 tablespoons extra-virgin olive oil
2 tablespoons (30 g) butter
Flaky salt, for finishing

Digby, Nova Scotia, sits on the southwest side of the province and is the scallop capital of the world. Rightly so. If you can find them for this dish, do! These particular gems are large, tender, and incredibly sweet in flavor. I don't see them all that often on the north shore, but when I do, you can be certain all other dinner plans go out the window and scallops are on the menu. When scallops are that fresh, you don't need to do much, but given this is a cookbook, I came up with a recipe should you want to try something new. I call for fennel pollen here, not to be faffy, but its delicate sweetness plays nicely with the nuttiness of the sesame seeds. However, it's not the end of the world if you don't have it. Serve with Tomato, Fennel, and White Bean Salad with Torn Bread and Smoky Aioli (page 76) or with whatever else you like.

METHOD

Season the scallops well on both sides with the fennel pollen (if using) and salt and pepper. Dip one side of the scallop in the sesame seeds, pressing firmly until evenly coated. Repeat with remaining scallops.

In a 12-inch (30 cm) skillet, heat the olive oil over medium-high heat until it shimmers. Add the scallops, sesame seed side down, and cook until golden brown and crispy on one side, 2 to 3 minutes. Flip and add the butter and as it melts, baste over the scallops until they are cooked through, 1 minute more. Season with flaky salt and divide among plates or assemble on a platter.

Poached Halibut *with* Fresh Chiles, Tomatoes, *and* Mint

SERVES
4

TIME
20 minutes

INGREDIENTS

1 ¼ pounds (570 g) halibut, cod, or haddock, cut into 4 pieces
Kosher salt and freshly ground black pepper
3 tablespoons extra-virgin olive oil, plus more for drizzling
2 large cloves garlic, thinly sliced
1 shallot, finely chopped
⅓ cup (30 g) finely chopped fennel
2 fresh chiles, such as cayenne or Fresno, thinly sliced (and seeded should you like)
½ teaspoon dried mint
1 ¼ pounds (570 g) mixed tomatoes, quartered if large and heirloom cherry tomatoes left whole
½ cup (120 ml) dry vermouth or white wine
¼ cup (13 g) torn mint leaves
¼ cup (10 g) torn basil leaves
Flaky salt, for finishing

I call for halibut in the recipe as it's readily available in Nova Scotia and it also happens to be one of my favorite fish. Cod and haddock will also work well. I enjoy making this in the summer with an assortment of colorful tomatoes in different shapes and sizes and when fresh chiles are in season. This recipe is dead simple and comes together in no time. Truthfully, I'm usually cooking it in my bathing suit after a day at the beach, so an olive oil piece of fried bread is generally the only other thing I can muster to serve it with and it's perfect. Should you want to make this dish in the winter, I'd swap my swimsuit for wool socks and use a can or two of cherry tomatoes in their juices and use red pepper flakes instead. The toast remains the same.

METHOD

Season the fish well with salt and pepper and set aside.

In a 12-inch (30 cm) sauté pan with a lid or a Dutch oven, heat the oil over medium heat until it shimmers. Add the garlic, shallot, fennel, and chiles. Cook, stirring occasionally, until they are softened but not taking on any color, 3 to 5 minutes. Season with salt. Add the dried mint and cook for 30 seconds more.

Add the tomatoes and season with salt. Cook, stirring occasionally, until they burst and start to become jammy, 5 to 7 minutes. I like some of the tomatoes to break down and some of them to retain some structure.

Add the vermouth and ¾ cup (180 ml) water and bring to a simmer. Gently add the fish and cover. Cook for 3 minutes. Remove from the heat and let sit for 4 to 5 minutes more. The residual heat will finish cooking the fish.

Transfer the fish and the tomatoes in their broth to a large shallow bowl or divide among four bowls, spooning any remaining broth on top. Top with the mint and basil, a drizzle of olive oil, and a few pinches of flaky salt.

Pan-Seared Trout *with* Corn Salad *and* Spicy Basil Dressing

SERVES
4

TIME
30 minutes

INGREDIENTS
for the corn salad:

- 2 tablespoons extra-virgin olive oil
- 1 small shallot, thinly sliced into rings
- 3 cups (435 g) corn kernels, raw or cooked (from 4 to 6 ears)
- Kosher salt and freshly ground black pepper
- 1 generous cup (30 g) loosely packed basil leaves, plus a few thinly sliced for garnish
- 1 generous cup (60 g) roughly chopped scallion greens
- 1 jalapeño, roughly chopped (seeded if you don't like things too spicy)
- 2 heaping tablespoons sour cream
- 2 tablespoons fresh lime juice, plus more as needed
- Flaky salt

for the fish:

- 4 skin-on trout fillets (6 to 8 ounces/170 to 225 g each)
- Kosher salt and freshly ground black pepper
- 2 tablespoons extra-virgin olive oil, plus more if needed
- Flaky salt

Trout is an easy-to-love fish. It's beautiful in color, relatively easy on the pocketbook, milder than salmon, and has a lovely sweetness to it. I kept the preparation of the trout simple and serve it with a snappy corn salad tossed in a slightly spicy basil dressing. It's very good. The beauty of this dish is that it's simple enough for the weeknight, but impressive looking enough for a dinner party. While trout is called for, you could easily substitute with arctic char or snapper.

METHOD

Make the corn salad: Heat a 12-inch (30 cm) skillet over medium heat for 1 to 2 minutes. Add the oil and when it simmers, add the shallot. Cook, stirring occasionally, until translucent, 2 minutes or so. Stir in the corn and cook, stirring occasionally, until it turns light golden in some spots, 4 to 5 minutes. Turn off the heat and season with salt and pepper. Allow the corn to come to room temperature.

Meanwhile, in a food processor, combine the basil, scallion greens, and jalapeño and pulse together until they are very fine. Add the sour cream and lime juice with a big pinch of kosher salt and pulse again until the dressing is loose enough that you could drizzle it. If it's not, stir in a few teaspoons of water. Taste and season with more salt if needed and then stir into the corn until well combined. Season with flaky salt and set aside.

Cook the fish: Pat the trout fillets very dry with a paper towel and season both sides with salt and pepper.

Heat a 12-inch (30 cm) nonstick skillet over medium-high heat for 1 to 2 minutes. Add the oil and when it shimmers, add 2 of the fillets skin side down, pressing them down with the back of a spatula so the skin gets as much contact with the pan as possible. Cook until it starts to brown around the edges and is nearly cooked through, 3 to 5 minutes. The flesh should look slightly opaque. Flip the fish and cook for about 30 seconds more until just cooked through. Repeat with remaining fillets, adding a bit more oil to the pan if needed. Remove from the heat and season with flaky salt.

To serve, divide the corn salad onto four plates or shallow bowls and top with a piece of trout, skin side up and a few thinly sliced basil leaves, if you're feeling fancy.

Your New Shrimp Scampi

SERVES
4

TIME
20 minutes

INGREDIENTS

- 2 tablespoons (30 g) unsalted butter
- 2 tablespoons extra-virgin olive oil
- 8 cloves garlic, crushed and skins removed
- 1 teaspoon red pepper flakes (or less if you'd prefer it less spicy)
- 1 lemon, thinly sliced, seeds removed
- Kosher salt
- ½ cup (120 ml) dry white wine
- 1½ pounds (680 g) large or extra-large shrimp, peeled and deveined
- 2 tablespoons roughly chopped fresh Italian parsley
- 2 tablespoons roughly chopped fresh mint
- Crusty bread, for serving

In my new take on this traditional recipe, I caramelize lemons in an ample amount of butter and oil, which results in a very bright and punchy version of this Italian American classic. You could toss the shrimp with pasta, but you don't have to. Crusty bread for dipping and a big salad would be my choice, with a big glass of red wine.

METHOD

In a 12-inch (30 cm) sauté pan, combine the butter, olive oil, garlic, pepper flakes, and lemon. Set over medium-low heat and cook, stirring occasionally, until the lemons start caramelizing and turning golden, 10 to 12 minutes. Season with salt.

Increase the heat to medium, add the wine, bring to a simmer, and cook until it is reduced by half, about 2 minutes.

Stir in the shrimp, season with salt, and toss until they are just cooked through, 2 to 3 minutes.

Transfer the shrimp to a plate and pour the sauce and lemons over top. Taste and season with salt as needed. Scatter with the parsley and mint and serve with crusty bread.

Fluke *with* Panko Walnut Crumbs *and* Broccolini

SERVES
4

TIME
20 minutes

INGREDIENTS

4 fluke fillets (5 to 6 ounces/140 to 170 g each); you can also use cod if easier to find
Kosher salt and freshly ground black pepper
1 cup (80 g) panko bread crumbs
¼ cup (30 g) finely chopped walnuts, hazelnuts, or almonds
3 teaspoons grated lemon zest
½ cup (25 g) loosely packed roughly chopped tarragon leaves
¼ cup (60 ml) extra-virgin olive oil

for the broccolini:
2 bunches broccolini, ends trimmed (about 1 pound/455 g total)
3 tablespoons olive oil
½ teaspoon red pepper flakes
Kosher salt and freshly ground black pepper
Lemon wedges, for serving

This is one of those easy, yet impressive dinners that comes together in no time and equals much more than the sum of its parts. If you can't find fluke, cod or haddock are good substitutes, and if you're not a tarragon fan (I'll never understand), feel free to swap in Italian parsley or cilantro. Serve with roasted potatoes or steamed rice.

METHOD

Preheat the oven to 425°F (220°C). Line a sheet pan with parchment paper.

Season the fluke well with salt and pepper and place on the lined sheet pan, leaving room for the broccolini.

In a medium bowl, combine the panko, walnuts, lemon zest, and tarragon. Pour in the olive oil and season with salt and pepper. Stir together until well combined. With a spoon top each piece of fish evenly with some of the panko mixture.

Prepare the broccolini: In a bowl, toss together the broccolini, olive oil, pepper flakes, and salt and black pepper to taste. Add it to the sheet pan around the fish.

Roast until the fish is opaque and the broccolini begins to turn golden around the edges and is bright in color, 10 to 15 minutes. Serve with lemon wedges.

Toasted Fregola *with* Scallops *and* Green Garlic Salsa Verde

SERVES
4

TIME
30 minutes

INGREDIENTS
for the salsa verde:
¼ cup (30 g) thinly sliced green garlic, or 2 cloves garlic, finely chopped
2 tablespoons finely chopped fresh parsley
2 tablespoons finely chopped fresh mint
2 tablespoons finely chopped garlic chives or regular chives
½ cup (120 ml) extra-virgin olive oil
Lemon juice
Kosher salt

for the fregola:
2 tablespoons extra-virgin olive oil
3 tablespoons finely chopped green garlic, or 2 cloves garlic, finely chopped
1 can (14.5 ounces/400 g) whole peeled tomatoes
Kosher salt
1 cup (225 g) fregola

for the scallops:
1 pound (455 g) sea scallops, patted dry
Kosher salt and freshly ground black pepper
2 tablespoons canola or vegetable oil
Chive blossoms (optional), for garnish
Flaky salt, for serving

I have an affection for fregola, any small pasta really, and I keep it on hand because it's super versatile. In the summer, I use it for salads and in the winter for brothy soups and stews. Here is its spring version: I've paired it with some seared scallops and a salsa verde made with green garlic in season. I wait all year for it! Green garlic is milder than its fully matured version, so feel free to use it liberally in place of regular garlic come May and June, or whenever it is spring where you are.

METHOD

Make the salsa verde: In a medium bowl, combine the green garlic, parsley, mint, and garlic chives. Pour in the olive oil, add a good squeeze of lemon juice, and season to taste with salt. Set aside.

Make the fregola: In a large Dutch oven, heat the olive oil over medium heat. Add the green or regular garlic and cook until golden, 1 to 2 minutes.

Add the tomatoes and crush them with a spatula or potato masher to loosen them up a bit. Season with salt, cover, and cook for 5 to 7 minutes to thicken it slightly.

Pour in 4 cups (960 ml) water and bring to a boil. Add the fregola and cook until al dente, 10 to 12 minutes.

When the pasta is nearly done, cook the scallops: Season the scallops well with salt and pepper. Heat a 12-inch (30 cm) cast-iron skillet over medium-high heat. Add the canola oil and when it shimmers, add the scallops. Cook undisturbed for 2 to 3 minutes, until they begin to brown and form a crust on the bottom. Flip the scallops to finish cooking, 1 to 2 minutes more.

To serve, ladle some of the saucy fregola into serving bowls, top each with a few of the scallops, and drizzle with the salsa verde and a few chopped chive blossoms (if using). Sprinkle with flaky salt.

A Note on Shellfish

I am not a soft-shell steamer clam person, and where we are in Nova Scotia, steamers—aka piss clams—are more readily available than the hard-shell (from the quahog family) type. So, I took it upon myself to find exactly what I was looking for, because a summer without clams prepared in many ways is no summer at all.

About a forty-five-minute drive from us in Malagash, Bay Enterprises, an oyster and quahog farm, sits right on the ocean. We'll often make a day trip to go see the Purdy family, whose family has been growing oysters there since 1867! Charles and his wife, Nancy, established the farm in 1974 and firmly believe in sustainable production, which I am thankful for, so I often call ahead to make sure they have what I need. Sometimes, due to high temperatures, vibrio (a natural bacteria in coastal waters) is present, which makes oysters and clams unsafe to sell, or rather they are unsafe to eat raw, so they don't take any chances. When they are open, they carry a number of hard-shell clams, such as littlenecks and cherrystones, as well as a wide variety of oysters; everything is mostly under a dollar each.

If you're lucky, Nancy Purdy will be there when you go. She's a gem and taught me that when the oysters are fresh they can actually live in the refrigerator for a good couple of weeks and stay perfectly edible. What a game changer! I always make sure to buy more than I need so I can whip out oysters on a random Tuesday evening while sipping a glass of rosé on the back porch. We've also used the pizza oven to make Oysters Rockefeller on a number of occasions. Clams Casino are also great pulled from the wood fire. And any night of the week is good for a dinner of fresh oysters and grilled sausages with good bread and butter. Blessed be the shellfish, they really do make everything more special.

A rosé day traveling through Cape Breton.

Buttery Basil *and* Lemon Grilled Clams

SERVES
4 as a light meal, 6 as a snack

TIME
20 minutes, plus dam soaking time

INGREDIENTS

2 dozen littleneck clams
Kosher salt
8 tablespoons (115 g/1 stick) unsalted butter, at room temperature
2 cups (80 g) loosely packed basil
2 teaspoons grated lemon zest
Lemon wedges, for serving
Toasted bread, for serving

If these clams don't scream summer, I'm not sure what will. We've got shellfish, a grill, and a dish to eat with your hands. The only thing missing is a cold beer. You might not use all the butter for this recipe, so feel free to store any leftover butter in the fridge for up to a week or freeze it and pull it out for a hit of sun in colder months. It works well stirred into pastas or on top of roasted or grilled vegetables, chicken, and fish.

METHOD

Soak the clams in a big pot of cold water with a few good pinches of kosher salt and let them sit for about 1 hour before cooking. This will help rid them of any grit. Drain and scrub the clams when you're ready to grill them or place them back in the fridge until you are.

Meanwhile, in a food processor, combine the butter, basil, and lemon zest and pulse together until combined. Transfer to a piece of plastic wrap and roll into a log-like shape and place in the fridge for 1 hour.

When you're ready to serve, make a hot fire in a charcoal grill or heat a gas grill to high.

Place the clams on the grill and when they sputter and pop open, 5 to 7 minutes, transfer to a plate. When cool enough to touch, remove their top shell and discard.

With a knife, top each of the clams with about ½ teaspoon of the butter. Use more should you like! Place the clams back on the grill and cook until the butter melts and starts to bubble. Transfer to a platter and serve with lemon wedges on the side and lots of toasted bread.

Seared Squid *with* Big Beans *and* Pancetta

SERVES
4

TIME
30 minutes

INGREDIENTS
for the beans:

- 4 ounces (115 g) pancetta, cut into ¼-inch (6 mm) dice
- 2 medium shallots, finely chopped
- 4 cloves garlic, finely chopped
- 2 tablespoons tomato paste
- ½ teaspoon red pepper flakes
- Kosher salt
- 2 cans (15 ounces/425 g each) butter beans, drained, or 3 cups (510 g) cooked beans
- ⅓ cup (75 ml) dry vermouth or white wine
- 2 ounces (55 g) baby arugula

for the squid:

- 1 pound (455 g) large squid (about 8), whole bodies (tubes) and tentacles, cleaned
- Kosher salt and freshly ground black pepper
- 2 tablespoons extra-virgin olive oil
- 3 tablespoons finely chopped fresh Italian parsley
- Grated zest of 1 medium lemon
- Flaky salt, for finishing

I feel squid is often overlooked, when in fact it is inexpensive, easy to prepare, and, as it is from the sea, it still feels special. I've paired it here with big, creamy beans, which is a nice contrast to both the crispiness of the salty pancetta and the squid, which is seared until golden brown. To make this dish pescatarian, simply leave out the pancetta. This squid works well as a main, but I could also see it served as part of a larger spread of dishes to graze on, including sautéed Broccoli Rabe with Toasted Garlic (page 232), Italian Shrimp Toast (page 22), Snacking Peppers (page 52), or even a bowl of spaghetti aglio olio. However you choose to serve it, I recommend having your fishmonger clean the squid for you; it's a real time-saver. Chilled red to drink, please.

METHOD

Line a plate with paper towels and have near the stove. In a 12-inch (30 cm) skillet, cook the pancetta over medium-low heat until the fat has rendered and the pancetta is golden and crispy, 5 to 7 minutes. Using a slotted spoon, transfer the pancetta to the paper towels, leaving rendered fat in the skillet.

Add the shallots and cook until softened, 4 to 6 minutes. Stir in the garlic, tomato paste, and pepper flakes and cook for 1 minute more. Season with salt. Add the beans and stir to coat with the onion mixture. Add the vermouth and bring to a boil. Cook until it's reduced about halfway, 2 minutes more. Return the pancetta to the skillet and stir to coat with the beans. Add the arugula to slightly wilt.

Meanwhile, cook the squid: Pat the squid very dry with paper towels and season well with salt and pepper. In a nonstick skillet, heat the olive oil over medium-high heat until it shimmers. Add the squid and cook, flipping once, until it takes on a golden color, 1 to 2 minutes per side. Transfer to a cutting board and cut the bodies into 1½- to 2-inch (4 to 5 cm) pieces, leaving the tentacles whole.

To serve, spoon the bean mixture onto a platter and top with the squid. Scatter the parsley and lemon zest over top and finish with a few pinches of flaky salt.

Harissa *and* Brown Sugar Glazed Salmon

SERVES
6 to 8

TIME
25 minutes

INGREDIENTS

2 salmon fillets (1 pound/ 455 g each)
Kosher salt
⅓ cup (90 g) harissa paste
1 tablespoon plus 1 teaspoon light brown sugar
2 cloves garlic, grated
2 tablespoons good-quality white wine vinegar
2 tablespoons extra-virgin olive oil
Flaky salt, for serving
¼ cup (12 g) roughly torn herbs, such as, dill, parsley, or sage, for serving

This simple salmon recipe has only a few ingredients and still manages to over-deliver on both flavor and presentation. I first made this dish for a big lunch that I was hosting at home with my wildly creative friends Dan Pelosi, Nicolette Miller, Paula, Kari, and Helen among them. Paula said it was the best salmon she's ever had! It is very good. I like serving this family-style at the table as it encourages conversation, especially if not everyone knows each other well. Think of it as a built-in ice breaker. Serve with Roasted Potato Salad with Za'atar, Feta, and Mint (page 66) and Little Gems with Avocado, Pistachios, and Miso-Honey Dressing (page 70).

METHOD

Preheat the oven to 400°F (200°C). Line a sheet pan with parchment paper.

Set the salmon on the sheet pan and season well all over with salt.

In a medium bowl, stir together the harissa paste, brown sugar, garlic, vinegar, and olive oil. Season with salt. Taste and adjust seasonings with more salt and vinegar as needed.

Pour over the salmon and with your hands or use a small spatula, coat the fish well with the marinade.

Bake until the salmon is cooked through and reaches an internal temperature of 145°F (63°C), 15 to 20 minutes.

Finish with a few pinches of flaky salt and the herbs and serve family-style at the table.

BRAISE, ROAST, SEAR

Roast Chicken *with* Lemon, Fennel, *and* Crispy Pecorino Potatoes

SERVES
4

TIME
1 hour

My family made a version of this recipe growing up and called it "Chicken Roti"—my guess is it was a play on the word rotisserie, I cannot confirm. Regardless, it was delicious and often served as part of our Christmas Day menu, where eating was an all-day affair. Multiple dishes would come out of the kitchen all afternoon into the evening. Eggplant Parm, roasted pork, a huge bowl of perfectly sauced ravioli, and on and on. My mama used bone-in chicken parts, but I've made some modifications including using a whole bird instead and also adding some fennel. Please note that not all the potatoes will be crispy at the end—they are not supposed to be. Some of them will be slick with lemony sauce, but I promise everyone will have a chance to get at a few bites of the craggy, crunchy bits. Serve with a big green salad tossed in Helen's Mustard Vinaigrette (page 234).

INGREDIENTS

1 whole chicken (3½ to 4 pounds/1.6 to 1.8 kg), backbone removed

Kosher salt and freshly ground black pepper

1 medium yellow onion, thinly sliced

1 small fennel bulb, thinly sliced

1½ pounds (680 g) russet potatoes, sliced into ¼-inch (6 mm) rounds

1 lemon, thinly sliced, seeds removed

1 cup (150 g) gently crushed Castelvetrano olives

¼ cup (60 ml) plus 2 tablespoons extra-virgin olive oil

1 cup (240 ml) dry white wine

2 ounces (55 g) grated pecorino or Parmesan cheese

2 tablespoons roughly chopped fresh Italian parsley

Flaky salt, for serving

METHOD

Preheat the oven to 425°F (220°C).

Season the chicken liberally with salt and pepper and set aside.

In a 12-inch (30 cm) cast-iron skillet or other deep sided ovenproof pan, combine the onion, fennel, potatoes, lemon, olives, and ¼ cup (60 ml) of the olive oil and season well with salt and pepper. Toss together until everything is well combined. Place the chicken on top of the potatoes and drizzle with the remaining 2 tablespoons olive oil.

Roast for 30 minutes. Add the wine to the pan, pouring it around the potatoes and fennel mixture and continue roasting until a meat thermometer inserted into the thickest part of the thigh registers 165°F (74°C), 15 to 20 minutes. Remove the chicken and tent with foil.

Return the potatoes to the oven and roast until fully cooked through, 5 to 10 minutes more.

Turn the oven to broil and scatter the grated cheese on top of the potatoes. Broil, watching closely, until the cheese begins to turn golden in spots and the edges of some of the potatoes and fennel turn crispy, 2 to 3 minutes. Remove from the oven and scatter the parsley over top.

Carve the chicken and serve the potatoes alongside with a few good pinches of flaky salt for both.

Lamb Chops *with a* Salad of Dates, Toasted Garlic, Walnuts, *and* Parsley

SERVES
4

TIME
25 minutes

INGREDIENTS

2 pounds (910 g) lamb loin chops (about 8 chops total)
Kosher salt and freshly ground black pepper
1 shallot, thinly sliced into rings
Juice of 1 lemon
2 tablespoons extra-virgin olive oil
¾ cup (110 g) roughly chopped dates, pits removed
⅓ cup (40 g) roughly chopped walnuts
4 cloves garlic, thinly sliced
½ teaspoon red pepper flakes
½ cup (25 g) roughly chopped fresh parsley
Flaky salt, for finishing

Nic-Nat farm up the road from our house in Nova Scotia has the most beautifully cut lamb chops I've ever seen, so I tend to stock up when we're there. The nice thing about loin chops is that they are one of the most tender parts of the lamb, cook quickly, and are incredibly flavorful. I simply season them with salt and pepper and use their leftover fat to warm the dates and toast the garlic and the walnuts, before tossing them with some quick pickled shallots for brightness.

METHOD

Bring the lamb to room temperature, if it is not already. Season liberally with salt and pepper and set aside.

In a small bowl, stir together the shallot and lemon juice and set aside.

Heat a 12-inch (30 cm) cast-iron skillet over medium-high heat. Add the oil and when it shimmers, add the lamb chops fat cap side down, pushing them together so they stand. Cook, allowing the fat to render and turn crispy and golden, about 3 minutes.

With tongs, move the chops flesh side down and cook, flipping once until a thermometer registers 135°F (57°C), about 2 minutes a side. Transfer to a plate.

Pour off all but 2 tablespoons of the fat from the skillet and set over medium heat. Add the dates, walnuts, garlic, and pepper flakes and cook, stirring frequently, until golden, about 3 minutes. Transfer the mixture to the bowl of shallots and add the parsley and any juices that have been distributed by the resting lamb chops. Stir together until combined. Taste and adjust seasoning with salt if needed.

Transfer the lamb chops to a plate or platter and spoon some of the salad over top with a few pinches of flaky salt. Pass the remaining salad at the table.

Date Night
Pork Chops *with* Mustard, Cream, *and* Cornichons

SERVES
2

TIME
20 minutes

INGREDIENTS

- 2 bone-in rib pork chops, each about 1½ inches (4 cm) thick
- Kosher salt and freshly ground black pepper
- 1½ tablespoons extra-virgin olive oil
- 1 small shallot, finely chopped
- ½ cup (120 ml) dry vermouth or white wine
- ½ cup (120 ml) heavy cream
- 1 tablespoon plus 1 teaspoon Dijon mustard
- 4 to 5 cornichons, finely chopped (2 tablespoons)
- 2 tablespoons finely chopped fresh parsley
- Flaky salt (optional), for serving

One unassuming Wednesday afternoon, Chad requested pork chops. We don't eat pork chops often (although we love them!), especially during the week, and it sounded like a nice thing to do. The weather was brisk and the first snow had arrived and I thought, heck, if I'm going to make chops, I'm going to make them worth my while. Initially, I thought to make this recipe with capers, but it's one of those ingredients that I always question if I have or not. I go back and forth from having numerous jars to zilch, which was the case this early December evening. Instead, I reached for cornichons, which *I do* always have in the fridge and knew would also add the briny punch I was looking for. I've never been so pleased to be out of capers! The cornichons are the secret for making this dish special, as well as the heavy cream of course. We made a fire, drank some wine, and toasted to good, spontaneous weeknight decadence.

METHOD

Pat the pork chops very dry and season well with salt and pepper.

Heat a heavy 10- or 12-inch (25 or 30 cm) skillet over medium-high heat for about 1 minute. Add the olive oil and when it shimmers, add the pork chops and cook undisturbed, until browned and golden on each slide, about 6 minutes total. Turn the pork onto its side so you can get the fat cap good and golden and cook 1 minute more. Transfer to a plate to rest.

Reduce the heat to medium. Add the shallot and cook until softened, about 1 minute. Season with salt. Add the vermouth, scraping up any browned bits that have formed at the bottom of the pan, until the liquid is reduced by half, about 2 minutes. Add the cream and mustard and stir until well combined. Simmer until the cream sauce begins to thicken slightly, about 3 minutes. Stir in the cornichons and parsley. Taste and season with more salt and pepper accordingly.

Slice the pork chops against the grain and transfer to a platter. Spoon the sauce over top with a pinch of flaky salt should you please.

STAUB

Chicken Pie *with* Buttered Toast Topping

SERVES
4

TIME
1 hour 20 minutes

INGREDIENTS
for the filling:
2 tablespoons extra-virgin olive oil
1 large leek, thinly sliced
12 ounces (340 g) mixed mushrooms, such as cremini and shiitake, torn into bite-size pieces
Kosher salt
2 cloves garlic, minced
2 tablespoons finely chopped fresh tarragon
2 tablespoons (30 g) butter
¼ cup (30 g) all-purpose flour
2 cups (480 ml) low-sodium chicken stock
¼ cup (60 ml) crème fraîche
3 cups (585 g) shredded cooked chicken
1 cup (135 g) frozen peas
¼ cup (15 g) finely chopped scallion greens
Grated zest of 1 lemon
Freshly ground black pepper

for the topping:
4 tablespoons (55 g) unsalted butter
8 slices white sandwich bread, such as Pepperidge Farm

This is undeniably a cheater's pot pie and I'm very pleased about it. Think of it as almost like creamed chicken under toast. You know I love toast. Eating at Woolworth's counter was before my time (although I'm sure it would have been a dream), and I imagine something like this would have been on the menu. I opt for a supermarket sandwich loaf, such as the Pepperidge Farm brand, but I'm sure an artisan Pullman bread would also work. Make sure you cut the slices thinly if you opt for the latter.

METHOD

Preheat the oven to 375°F (190°C).

Make the filling: In a medium skillet, heat the olive oil over medium heat until it shimmers. Add the leeks and cook until they begin to soften, 3 to 4 minutes. Add the mushrooms and cook until they release their liquid, 10 to 12 minutes. Season with salt. Stir in the garlic and the tarragon and cook for 1 minute more.

Add the butter and once it melts, sprinkle the flour over the vegetables, stirring them to coat. Gradually stir in the stock ½ cup (120 ml) or so at a time, whisking out any lumps. Bring to a simmer and cook until it begins to slightly thicken, about 2 minutes.

Remove from the heat and stir in the crème fraîche, followed by the chicken, peas, scallion greens, and lemon zest. Stir until everything is combined. Taste and adjust seasonings, as needed, with salt and freshly ground pepper.

Transfer the mixture to an 8-cup (2 L) gratin dish.

Make the topping: In a saucepan, melt the butter over medium-low heat. Remove from the heat. Piece by piece, dip the bread on one side to coat in the butter. Transfer to a cutting board and cut each slice on the diagonal. Shingle the bread over top of the filling to cover the surface, overlapping as you work.

Bake until the bread is golden brown and the filling is bubbling, 15 to 20 minutes.

Allow the pie to cool for 10 minutes before serving.

Spiced Lamb *and* Lemon Skewers *with* Cucumber and Sumac

SERVES
4 to 6

TIME
30 minutes, plus marinating time

INGREDIENTS
for the lamb:

1½ pounds (680 g) boneless leg of lamb, cut into 1½-inch (4 cm) pieces
1½ teaspoons kosher salt
2 teaspoons dried mint
2 teaspoons ground turmeric
1½ teaspoons ground cumin
1 teaspoon Aleppo pepper or ½ teaspoon red pepper flakes
½ teaspoon ground cinnamon
3 cloves garlic, grated
¼ cup (60 ml) extra-virgin olive oil
10 to 15 pitted dates
1 medium red onion, cut into small wedges
1 large lemon, cut into small wedges

for the labneh:

2 cups (480 ml) labneh or sour cream
2 tablespoons fresh lemon juice
Kosher salt
1 tablespoon za'atar
2 tablespoons finely chopped fresh herbs, such as dill, parsley, or cilantro
Olive oil, for drizzling
Flaky salt (optional), for finishing

for the cucumbers:

6 Persian (mini) cucumbers, thinly sliced lengthwise
Kosher salt
1 tablespoon fresh lemon juice
2 teaspoons ground sumac
¼ cup (10 g) roughly chopped tender herbs, such as cilantro, mint, and dill

This feast is perfect for christening grill season. In fact, the first time I made it was at the start of grilling season, and it reminded me how creative you can get threading things onto skewers! If you have more time to let the lamb marinate, it will deepen the flavor, but if you've only got an hour, it will do. I highly recommend making Homemade Flatbread (page 226) for this meal. It's incredibly satisfying. If you don't eat lamb, like my friend Kevin, you can still make this recipe. Try it with beef or chicken; and if you do, go with fattier cuts such as boneless short ribs and chicken thighs. He did and was very pleased.

METHOD

Marinate the lamb: In a large bowl, combine the lamb, salt, mint, turmeric, cumin, Aleppo pepper, cinnamon, and garlic. Add the olive oil and stir everything together until the lamb is well coated in the spice mixture. Refrigerate for at least 1 hour and up to overnight. Take the lamb out of the refrigerator about 1 hour before serving to come to room temperature.

Meanwhile, prepare the labneh: In a bowl, stir together the labneh, lemon juice, and a good pinch of salt. Taste and adjust with more salt as needed. Top with the za'atar, herbs, a good drizzle of olive oil, and a few pinches of flaky salt (if using).

Prepare the cucumbers: Place the cucumbers in a large bowl and season generously with salt and the lemon juice. Taste and adjust seasonings with more salt and lemon juice as needed. Transfer to a platter and top with the sumac and the herbs.

When ready to finish, build a screaming hot fire or if using gas, take it as hot as it will go.

Thread the lamb onto a 9- or 10-inch (23- or 25-cm) skewer, followed by a date, a piece of onion, and a piece of lemon. Repeat with the remaining ingredients, making 4 skewers total. Brush each skewer with a bit of olive oil.

Grill the skewers, flipping occasionally, until the lamb is brown and golden, about 6 minutes total for medium-rare. Transfer to a plate or platter.

Serve with the labneh alongside as well as grilled flatbreads or pita.

Piccata-Like Chicken *with* Olives *and* Chiles

SERVES
4

TIME
30 minutes

INGREDIENTS

1½ pounds (680 g) boneless, skinless chicken thighs

1½ teaspoons kosher salt

½ cup (65 g) all-purpose flour

3 tablespoons extra-virgin olive oil, plus more if needed

½ to 1 teaspoon red pepper flakes, to taste

½ cup (120 ml) dry white wine or dry vermouth

½ cup (120 ml) chicken stock

1 large Meyer or regular lemon, half thinly sliced (seeds removed), half juiced (which should yield 4 tablespoons)

½ cup (80 g) Castelvetrano olives, thwacked with the side of knife and pits removed

4 tablespoons (60 g) cold butter, cut into pieces

2 to 3 tablespoons roughly chopped fresh Italian parsley

Flaky salt and freshly ground black pepper (optional)

This recipe is a twist on the Italian American classic, which I also love, but this is equally good. I swapped capers for buttery Castelvetrano olives and added some heat. I usually buy olives with their pits intact; if you have ones where they are removed, give them a very rough chop. I love making this dish in winter months, because Meyer lemons are in season and they are sweeter and a bit less acidic than normal lemons, and you can eat them peel and all. Their brightness is a welcome jolt to the palate on cold, gray days. Serve with Butter Rice with Roasted Tomatoes and Herbs (page 58).

METHOD

Lightly pound the chicken thighs between sheets of parchment paper until they are about ½ inch (12 mm) thick. Season with the kosher salt.

Place the flour in a large shallow bowl. Working with one at a time, dredge each cutlet through the flour to coat. Shake off any excess flour and transfer to a large plate or platter.

In a large skillet, heat the oil over medium-high heat. Working in batches to not crowd the pan, use tongs to add the cutlets to the pan away from you. Cook until they begin to brown on the bottom, 3 to 4 minutes. Flip and cook until just cooked through, an additional 2 to 3 minutes. Transfer to a platter.

Reduce the heat to medium. Add the pepper flakes and cook until fragrant, about 30 seconds. Add the wine and bring to a simmer, scraping up any of the browned bits that have formed on the bottom of the pan, and simmer until reduced by half, about 2 minutes. Add the chicken stock, lemon slices, lemon juice, and olives and simmer until reduced by half, about 2 minutes more.

Whisk in the butter until the sauce is glossy. Return the chicken to the pan, toss it to coat in the sauce, and simmer until it thickens slightly, 1 to 2 minutes more.

Transfer to a platter and spoon the sauce over top of the chicken and top with the parsley. Season with flaky salt and black pepper if you like.

Lamb Meatballs *with* Mint and Feta *in* Saucy Couscous

SERVES
4

TIME
45 minutes

INGREDIENTS
for the meatballs:
1 pound (455 g) ground lamb
1½ ounces (40 g) feta cheese, crumbled
½ cup (40 g) panko bread crumbs
¼ cup (13 g) finely chopped fresh parsley
½ medium yellow onion, grated
3 cloves garlic, finely chopped
1 large egg
1½ teaspoon dried mint
1 teaspoon ground cumin
½ teaspoon ground cinnamon
1 teaspoon salt
2 tablespoons extra-virgin olive oil

for the couscous:
2 tablespoons extra-virgin olive oil
6 cloves garlic, roughly chopped
2 teaspoons ground turmeric
¼ cup (60 g) harissa paste
2 tablespoons tomato paste
4 cups (950 ml) chicken broth
2 cups (400 g) pearled couscous
Kosher salt

for serving:
Crumbled feta cheese
¼ cup (10 g) roughly chopped fresh cilantro, mint, or dill, or combination of all three
Flaky salt (optional)

This one-pot dish couldn't be more comforting on a brisk night served with a bright green salad. If you don't feel like pan-frying the meatballs, you could very mildly dirty a sheet pan and cook them at 425°F (220°C) in the oven for about 10 minutes. Alternatively, meatballs turn out beautifully when cooked in an air fryer, should you have one and feel like breaking it out. I often do.

METHOD

Make the meatballs: In a large bowl, combine the lamb, feta, panko, parsley, onion, garlic, egg, mint, cumin, cinnamon, and salt and mix together until well combined. With damp hands, roll the lamb mixture into small balls, about 1½ inches (4 cm) in diameter; it should yield 16 to 20 meatballs.

In a large Dutch oven, heat the olive oil over medium heat until it shimmers. Working in batches to avoid overcrowding, brown the meatballs, 5 to 7 minutes total and set aside. They may not be cooked all the way through and that is okay; they will finish cooking in the sauce.

Make the saucy couscous: Wipe out the Dutch oven if needed and heat over medium heat. Add the olive oil and when it shimmers add the garlic and cook until fragrant, 1 to 2 minutes. Add the turmeric, harissa paste, and tomato paste and cook until the tomato and harissa paste begin to get slightly toasty, about 2 minutes more. Add the broth and bring to a boil, followed by the couscous, and cook according to the package directions.

About 5 minutes before the couscous is done, gently stir in the reserved meatballs and any juices that have accumulated. Taste and adjust seasonings with salt as needed.

To serve: Ladle into bowls and top with a bit of feta and the herbs. Finish with a good pinch of flaky salt if you like.

A Very Spiced Chicken *with* Cippolinis *and* Preserved Lemon *and* Date Relish

SERVES
4

TIME
1 hour 15 minutes

INGREDIENTS
for the chicken and onions:
3½ teaspoons kosher salt
1 teaspoon freshly ground black pepper
1 tablespoon za'atar
1 teaspoon ground turmeric
½ teaspoon ground cinnamon
½ teaspoon red pepper flakes
1 whole chicken (3½ to 4 pounds/1.6 to 1.8 kg), backbone removed
Olive oil spray
1 pound (455 g) cipollini onions, peeled
2 tablespoons extra-virgin olive oil

for the relish:
⅓ cup (50 g) roughly chopped pitted dates
¼ cup (50 g) chopped preserved lemon, both flesh and rind, seeds removed
¼ cup (10 g) chopped fresh cilantro
2 tablespoons roughly chopped fresh mint
1 clove garlic, grated
½ cup (120 ml) olive oil
Kosher salt

This is a very good chicken recipe. I've made it a few times and I stand by my conviction. I opted to cook the bird at a lower temperature than I normally would and because there is a lot of spice going on, you will get a juicy bird and a crusty skin. I also call for olive oil spray, which is something I never thought to do before. I intended to drizzle the oil on top of the bird to prevent the spices from scorching, but I saw a can of California Olive Oil spray staring at me and a lightbulb went off. Using it gives you incredibly even coverage! Try it and see. The relish is also delicious. Taste it before adding additional salt, as preserved lemon is pretty salty already.

METHOD

Preheat the oven to 350°F (180°C).

Prepare the chicken: In a small bowl, stir together the salt, black pepper, za'atar, turmeric, cinnamon, and pepper flakes. Season the chicken on both sides evenly and place on a sheet pan. Spray the top of the bird with the olive oil spray in an even layer. Let the chicken hang out while the oven comes to temperature.

Transfer the bird to the oven, legs toward the back, and roast for 30 minutes.

Meanwhile, in a small bowl, toss the cippolini onions with the olive oil and season with salt.

After the chicken has been roasting for about 30 minutes, scatter the onions around the bird, return to the oven, and roast until a thermometer registers 165°F (74°C) in the thigh, about 30 minutes more. Check the onions occasionally and toss to make sure they aren't burning. The onions should be schmaltzy and softened. Remove from the oven and let the chicken rest for at least 10 minutes.

While the chicken cooks, make the relish: In a medium bowl, combine the dates, preserved lemon, cilantro, mint, garlic, and olive oil and stir together until well combined. Taste and adjust seasoning with salt if needed.

Carve the bird and pass the relish at the table to spoon on top.

Coconut *and* Ginger Braised Short Ribs *with* Mustard Greens

SERVES
4 to 6

TIME
2½ to 3 hours

INGREDIENTS

3 to 4 pounds (1.4 to 1.8 kg) English-style bone-in beef short ribs, cut into 3-inch (7.5 cm) segments, patted very dry
3 to 4 teaspoons kosher salt
Freshly ground black pepper
2 tablespoons canola or other neutral oil
1 piece (3-inch/7.5 cm) fresh ginger, grated (about 2 tablespoons)
6 cloves garlic, grated
3 shallots, finely chopped
3 Thai bird's eye chiles, thinly sliced
1 tablespoon tomato paste
½ cup (120 ml) dry sherry or white wine
1 can (13.5 ounces/400 ml) full-fat coconut milk
2 cups (480 ml) beef stock
2 tablespoons light brown sugar
5 cups (350 g) roughly chopped mustard greens, kale, or Swiss chard
Grated zest and juice of 1 lime

for serving:
Steamed jasmine rice
Roughly chopped cilantro (optional)
Thinly sliced scallions (optional)
Fried Shallots (optional; page 233)

Short ribs are browned and braised in a fragrant broth of coconut milk studded with ginger, garlic, and Thai chiles. They are perfect for a winter dinner party and can be made up to 2 days in advance (up until adding your greens), should that be of help. Simply bring to room temperature and warm gently on the stove, and when warm, add the greens to wilt. This dish begs to be served in bowls over steamed rice, and although I listed toppings as optional, they are highly recommended for vibrancy and texture. You can thank me later.

METHOD

Preheat the oven to 350°F (180°C).

Season the short ribs with the kosher salt and pepper on all sides. If you can do this overnight and leave them uncovered in the fridge, good for you; if not, move on!

In a large Dutch oven or other ovenproof pot, heat the oil over medium-high heat until it shimmers. Working in batches, if necessary, to avoid overcrowding, sear the short ribs, turning occasionally, until golden and browned all over, 8 to 10 minutes. Transfer to a plate, leaving the fat behind.

Reduce the heat to medium-low and stir in the ginger, garlic, shallots, and chiles and cook, stirring occasionally, until softened, but without taking on any color, 3 minutes or so. Add the tomato paste and stir to incorporate. Add the sherry and scrape up any browned bits that have formed at the bottom of the pan and cook to reduce the mixture by half, about 2 minutes.

Stir in the coconut milk and beef stock and bring to a simmer. Add the brown sugar and stir until it dissolves. Nestle the short ribs back into the pot and cover. Transfer to the oven and braise the short ribs until the meat is tender and falling off the bone and the liquid is thickened, 2 to 2½ hours.

When ready to serve, slip the meat off the bones and shred into the pot. Over low heat, add the greens and stir until they are wilted. Add the lime zest and lime juice. Taste and adjust seasoning with salt if needed.

Serve over rice in bowls. If desired, top with cilantro, scallions, and fried shallots.

Pork Schnitzel *and* Crunchy Cabbage *with* Tahini, Yogurt, *and* Dill Dressing

SERVES
4

TIME
35 minutes

INGREDIENTS
for the salad and dressing:

- ¾ cup (180 ml) whole-milk Greek yogurt
- ¼ cup (55 ml) tahini
- 1 clove garlic, grated
- 2 tablespoons warm water, plus more as needed
- 2 tablespoons fresh lemon juice, plus more as needed
- Kosher salt and freshly ground black pepper
- 5 cups (350 g) thinly sliced savoy or napa cabbage
- ½ medium white onion, thinly sliced
- 1 cup (40 g) loosely packed roughly chopped fresh dill
- 2 tablespoons toasted sesame seeds
- Flaky salt, for finishing

for the schnitzel:

- ½ cup (65 g) all-purpose flour
- 2 large eggs, whisked with a small splash of water
- 2¼ cups (180 g) panko bread crumbs
- Kosher salt and freshly ground black pepper
- 4 boneless pork tenderloin cutlets or boneless chops (5 ounces/140 g each), pounded ⅛ inch (3 mm) thick
- Peanut or canola oil, for frying
- Flaky salt
- Lemon wedges, for serving

Here's a good tip: Always make friends with your butcher. They are genuinely curious about what you're making with your purchases and like talking through recipe ideas, and can steer you in the right direction should you have questions. Chances are they will also be delighted and enthusiastic about pounding pork chops to your desired thickness upon request, which in the case of this recipe will also save you time. If you don't eat pork, feel free to swap in chicken breasts. And because "crispy loves creamy," a motto I live by, the crunchy cabbage salad with tahini and yogurt dressing makes a perfect counterbalance to the golden-brown, shallow-fried schnitzel.

METHOD

Make the salad: In a medium bowl, whisk together the yogurt, tahini, garlic, water, and lemon juice and season with some salt and pepper. If needed, whisk in a few more tablespoons of warm water to loosen it up a bit, taste and adjust seasonings with more lemon juice and salt if you please.

In a large bowl, toss together the cabbage, onion, and dill and season well with salt and pepper. Pour in the salad dressing and toss again to make sure everything is well coated. Top with the sesame seeds and finish with a good pinch of flaky salt. Set aside.

Make the schnitzel: Set up a dredging station in three shallow bowls: Add the flour to one, the eggs to a second, and the panko to the third. Season each with a good pinch of salt and pepper.

Season the pork well with salt and pepper. Using one hand for wet and the other for dry, dip each cutlet into the flour, shaking off any excess, followed by the egg mixture, then the panko, pressing to make sure it gets good coverage. Transfer to a plate or platter.

Line a baking sheet or large platter with paper towels and have near the stove. Pour ⅛ inch (3 mm) oil into a 12-inch (30 cm) skillet and heat over medium-high heat until it shimmers. Add a pinch of the panko—if it sizzles your oil is hot enough. Add 2 of the cutlets and press with the back of the spatula to ensure even browning. Cook, flipping once, until golden brown and cooked through, 2 to 3 minutes per side. Transfer to the paper towels and season immediately with flaky salt. If the oil starts to smoke, reduce the heat to medium. Repeat with the remaining cutlets, adding more oil if the pan starts to look dry.

Divide the pork among plates and serve with a wedge of lemon and the cabbage salad.

Calabrian Chili *and* Pickled Pepper–Braised Pork *in* Tomato

SERVES
6 to 8

TIME
3 to 3 ½ hours

INGREDIENTS

- 5 to 5 ½ pounds (2.3 to 2.5 kg) boneless pork shoulder
- 5 teaspoons kosher salt
- 2 tablespoons extra-virgin olive oil
- 1 medium onion, finely chopped
- 8 cloves garlic, smashed and peeled
- 1 tablespoon tomato paste
- 1 heaping tablespoon Calabrian chili paste
- 1 heaping tablespoon hoagie spread or finely chopped pickled peppers
- 2 tablespoons roughly chopped mixed fresh herbs, such as rosemary, sage, or thyme
- 1 jar (24.5 ounces/700 g) passata
- Creamy Polenta (page 236), for serving

I first made this dish when my dad and family came for their annual holiday visit and it was a *big* hit. Not to toot my own horn or anything, but this pork is insanely good. It gets great heat from the Calabrian chilies, and the pickled peppers provide delicate acidity. I call for Cento hoagie spread here, because it's always in my fridge. If you can't find it, finely chop any pickled pepper of your choosing, but also buy the hoagie spread! It's really good. If you can get ahead of it and make the pork a few days in advance, it will only deepen the dish's flavor and make it even more delectable! I highly recommend serving it over creamy polenta, to which I add lots of butter and mascarpone. A side of blanched broccoli rabe tossed with oil and toasted garlic never hurt anyone either.

METHOD

Preheat the oven to 350°F (180°C).

Season the pork all over with the salt. If you can do this a day in advance and leave it uncovered in the fridge, great. If not, carry on, it will be fine!

In a large Dutch oven, heat the oil over medium heat until it shimmers. Add the pork and brown it well on all sides, 12 to 15 minutes total. Remove the pork and set aside.

Pour off all but 2 tablespoons of fat from the pot. Add the onion and garlic and stir to coat in the oil. Cook until the onion begins to soften and the garlic turns golden, 2 to 3 minutes. Season with salt.

Add the tomato paste and toast for 1 to 2 minutes. Stir in the Calabrian chili paste, hoagie spread, and herbs and cook for 1 minute more. Pour in the passata and then fill the jar one-quarter of the way up with water, swish around to loosen up any remaining sauce, and add to the pot. Bring the mixture to a simmer, return the pork to the pot, cover, and transfer to the oven.

Braise until the pork is melting tender, 3 to 3½ hours.

Shred the pork directly in the sauce. Taste and adjust the season with more salt if needed. Serve over the creamy polenta.

Battered Pecorino Cutlets *with* Sungolds *and* Crushed Olive Salsa

SERVES
4

TIME
40 minutes

INGREDIENTS
for the chicken:

2 boneless, skinless chicken breasts (about 12 ounces/ 340 g each)
Kosher salt
3 large eggs
⅓ cup (30 g) grated pecorino cheese (I like Locatelli)
¼ cup (10 g) finely chopped fresh parsley
Freshly ground black pepper
1 cup (125 g) all-purpose flour for dredging
⅔ cup (160 ml) extra-virgin olive oil, for shallow-frying
Flaky salt

for the salsa:

2 pints (600 g) Sungold or other small, pretty tomato varieties, halved
1 cup (155 g) Castelvetrano olives, crushed with the side of a knife and pitted
1 small red onion, thinly sliced
¼ cup (13 g) parsley leaves
¼ cup (60 ml) olive oil
2 teaspoons sherry vinegar, plus more to taste
Kosher salt and freshly ground black pepper
Flaky salt, for serving

Chicken cutlets are upgraded and battered in an egg and cheese mixture that is almost Francese-like and deeply savory. The cutlets shallow-fry until they are golden, and the bright tomatoes and olive salsa that they're topped with gives them a nice jolt of acidity. I call for Sungolds here, which are readily available in the summertime. If you find yourself in another season, grape or cherry tomatoes will also work well.

METHOD

With a sharp knife, starting on a fat side of the breast, slice each chicken breast horizontally in half to get 2 cutlets each, or a total of 4. Place a piece of parchment or plastic over top of the chicken and pound with a mallet or a rolling pin until they are about ¼ inch (6 mm) thick. Season with salt.

In a wide shallow bowl, whisk together the egg, pecorino, and parsley and season lightly with salt (the pecorino is salty already) and black pepper. Add the flour to another wide shallow bowl.

Line a plate with paper towels and have near the stove. In a 12-inch (30 cm) skillet, heat the oil over medium heat until it shimmers. Test to make sure the olive oil is hot enough by adding a few pinches of flour—when they sizzle, you're ready.

Working one at a time, dredge a cutlet in the flour, shaking any excess off, and then dip into the egg and cheese mixture and add to the pan away from you. You should be able to get 2 in the pan at once. Cook until the outside is golden and the chicken is cooked through, 3 to 4 minutes per side. Transfer the chicken to the paper towels and sprinkle with flaky salt. Repeat with the remaining 2 cutlets, adding a bit more oil if the pan is looking dry.

Make the salsa: In a large bowl, combine the tomatoes, olives, onion, and parsley leaves. Stir in the olive oil and vinegar and season with salt and pepper. Taste and adjust with more vinegar and salt as needed.

Transfer the cutlets to a large platter and spoon the salsa over top and finish with a few pinches of flaky salt.

Roast Chicken "Romesco" *with* Pearled Couscous

SERVES
6

TIME
40 minutes

INGREDIENTS
for the chicken and the couscous:
8 bone-in, skin-on chicken thighs (about 6½ ounces/185 g each)
1½ tablespoons smoked paprika
Kosher salt and freshly ground black pepper
4 tablespoons (60 ml) canola or other high-heat oil
1 medium leek, thinly sliced into rounds and well rinsed
6 cloves garlic, roughly chopped
1½ cups (300 g) pearled couscous
2 cups (480 ml) chicken stock

for the romesco:
1½ cups (360 g) finely chopped roasted red peppers
½ teaspoon red pepper flakes
1 large clove garlic, grated
3 tablespoons extra-virgin olive oil
1½ tablespoons sherry vinegar
¼ cup (13 g) Italian parsley, finely chopped
Kosher salt
Flaky salt, for serving

Chicken thighs and pearled couscous make for a perfect cozy, one-pan weeknight meal that still feels elevated enough to serve at a dinner party. Bone-in chicken thighs are simply seasoned with smoked paprika, salt, and pepper and then seared until golden. You finish the cooking process by roasting them in the oven to keep their crispy skin. A play on romesco turns the classic Spanish sauce into more of a salsa-like condiment, which is served alongside. It would also work well spooned over roasted or grilled fish. Serve with a big green salad, tossed with fennel and shaved Manchego.

METHOD

Preheat the oven to 350°F (180°C).

Prepare the chicken: Season the chicken thighs evenly with the smoked paprika, salt, and pepper

In a large Dutch oven, heat 2 tablespoons of the oil over medium-high heat until it shimmers, Working in batches to avoid overcrowding, add the chicken skin side down and cook undisturbed until the skin is golden brown, 5 to 6 minutes. Flip and repeat cooking 5 minutes more. Transfer to a plate.

Wipe out the pan. Reduce the heat to medium-low and heat the remaining 2 tablespoons of oil. Add the leeks and cook, stirring frequently, until softened, 2 to 3 minutes more. Season with salt. Add the garlic and cook for 1 minute more. Add the couscous, toss to coat, and toast with the leeks and the garlic, 2 minutes more. Pour in the stock, bring to a simmer, and cook until about half the stock is absorbed, about 5 minutes. Nestle the chicken back into the pan and transfer to the oven.

Bake until the chicken is cooked through, 10 to 15 minutes.

Meanwhile, make the romesco: In a medium bowl, stir together the roasted red peppers, pepper flakes, garlic, olive oil, vinegar, and parsley and season with salt. Taste and adjust seasonings to your preference with a bit more salt and vinegar as needed.

Spoon the sauce over the top of the chicken and couscous and pass more at the table. Finish with a few pinches of flaky salt.

A LITTLE SOMETHING SWEET

Rye Blueberry Galette

SERVES
4 to 6

TIME
3 hours (includes chilling time)

INGREDIENTS
for the dough:
1 cup (125 g) all-purpose flour
1 cup (100 g) rye flour
1½ teaspoons kosher salt
1 tablespoon sugar
12 tablespoons (170 g/1½ sticks) very cold unsalted butter, cut into pieces
¼ cup (60 ml) ice water

for the filling:
1 pint (340 g) blueberries
2 teaspoons cornstarch
¼ cup (50 g) granulated sugar, plus more if needed
½ teaspoon vanilla extract
1 teaspoon grated citrus zest
Lemon or lime juice
Pinch of kosher salt
1 large egg, whisked
Demerara sugar for sprinkling
Ice cream or whipped cream, for serving

This forgiving dessert makes anyone intimated by baking feel like a pro. It couldn't be simpler to pull together. In true Colu fashion, I kept the filling somewhat up to interpretation. I trust you'll figure it out and tweak it to your liking. If you can find it, I love using a combination of white and rye flour, but subbing wheat flour for the rye will also work. The rye flour gives the galette a nuttier tasting crust. I can't stop making galettes and have no intention of stopping anytime soon. I hope you'll join me.

METHOD

Make the dough: In a food processor, pulse together the all-purpose flour, rye flour, salt, and sugar to combine. Add the butter and pulse a few times until the mixture resembles coarse meal with a few quarter-size pieces still intact.

Transfer the mixture to a lightly floured work surface and drizzle with the ice water. With your hands, gently knead together the dough, adding more ice water by the tablespoonful as needed, until no dry spots remain (do not overwork). Pat into a disk and wrap in plastic. Refrigerate for at least 2 hours and up to 3 days.

Preheat the oven to 400°F (200°C).

Make the filling: In a large bowl, stir together the blueberries, cornstarch, sugar, vanilla, citrus zest, a good squeeze of lemon or lime juice, and the kosher salt. Taste and add a bit more sugar if needed—this will depend on the sweetness of your fruit.

Take the dough out of the refrigerator and let it sit for 5 minutes. Unwrap the dough and roll out on a lightly floured sheet of parchment paper to a 12- to 14-inch (30 to 35 cm) round about ⅛ inch (3 mm) thick. Transfer on the parchment to a baking sheet.

Add the berry mixture to the center of the dough, leaving a 2-inch (5 cm) border all around. Fold the dough up and over the edge of the filling, pleating the dough as you go around. Brush the crust with the egg and scatter the demerara sugar over top.

Bake the galette until the crust is golden brown and cooked through, 40 to 45 minutes, rotating the pan halfway through.

Let cool on the baking sheet for 1 hour before serving with the ice cream or whipped cream, if desired.

Crumbly Apple Cake *with* Fennel Seeds

SERVES
8

TIME
45 minutes

INGREDIENTS

- 1 teaspoon fennel seeds
- 8 tablespoons (115 g/1 stick) unsalted butter, at room temperature
- ¾ cup (165 g) packed light brown sugar
- 1 cup (125 g) whole wheat flour, sifted
- 1 teaspoon baking powder
- Generous pinch of kosher salt
- ⅛ teaspoon freshly grated nutmeg
- 2 large eggs
- 1 tart apple, such as Pink Lady or Cortland, thinly sliced into wedges, about ¼ inch thick
- Demerara sugar and lemon juice, for topping
- Softly whipped cream or ice cream (optional), for serving

This recipe is inspired by Marian Burrows's famous Plum Torte. My version is nuttier from the use of whole wheat flour, and I also use light brown sugar instead of white, which deepens the color and adds density. I did all of this by hand with a wooden spoon at the farmhouse where tools are sparse, but you could also use a stand mixer to beat it. The texture is almost crusty and crumbly, which is right up my alley. Serve with softly whipped cream or ice cream or alongside a cup of your morning coffee.

METHOD

Preheat the oven to 350°F (180°C).

Spritz an 8- or 9-inch (20 or 23 cm) springform pan with cooking spray.

In a small skillet, toast the fennel seeds over medium heat, stirring occasionally, until fragrant, 3 to 5 minutes. Once cooled, pound in a mortar and pestle or blitz in a spice grinder and set aside.

In a bowl, cream the butter and brown sugar together and stir in the fennel seeds. Add the flour, baking powder, salt, nutmeg, and eggs and stir until well combined.

Spoon the batter into the springform pan and press it down so it is evenly distributed. Place the apple slices skin side up on top. Sprinkle with demerara sugar, followed by a good squeeze of lemon juice.

Bake until a toothpick inserted in the center of the cake comes out clean, 30 to 35 minutes.

Let the cake cool in the pan for 10 to 15 minutes on a wire rack. Serve warm or at room temperature, with ice cream or whipped cream, if desired.

A Brandy Alexander

MAKES
1 cocktail

TIME
5 minutes

INGREDIENTS

Ice
1½ ounces Cognac or brandy
1 ounce dark crème de cacao
1 ounce heavy cream
Freshly grated nutmeg, for serving

I bartended in restaurants all through college and again when I first moved to New York City in the early aughts. So as you can imagine, it was the last thing I wanted to do when I went home for the holidays. Yet, somehow I always ended up in the kitchen, shaker in hand, making Brandy Alexanders to order. I wasn't thrilled. It took me up until meeting our pal Dan Farber, an incredibly talented brandy distiller, to think about them again. Upon our first meeting, trying to make conversation, I sheepishly asked how he felt about this classic, retro dessert cocktail. I was surprisingly met with warm enthusiasm and promptly invited him over to drink one. He did. We were up till 1 a.m.

METHOD

Fill a cocktail or coupe glass with ice water. In a cocktail shaker, combine the Cognac, crème de cacao, and cream, and fill with ice. Shake with great purpose until the outside of the shaker becomes so cold you almost cannot touch it. Discard the ice water from the cocktail glass and strain the cocktail into the glass. Grate a bit of nutmeg over the top.

Sherry Affogato

SERVES
1

TIME
5 minutes

INGREDIENTS

- 2 medium scoops vanilla ice cream
- 1½ ounces Pedro Ximénez sherry
- Flaky salt
- Shortbread (store-bought is fine!), for serving

It's no secret that we love sherry in this house. Chad and I can easily go through a large bottle of La Guita on a hot afternoon with a bag of potato chips. After sampling each kind of sherry for this dessert—a very tough job, I might add—in the end, we decided that Pedro Ximénez was the one. It's nutty, sweet, and tastes of dried fruit, and it pairs exceptionally well with vanilla ice cream. This is of course inspired by the Italian after-dinner treat of pouring espresso over vanilla ice cream. *Affogato* translates to "drowning" in English, so that applies here, too.

METHOD

Add the ice cream to a small clear drinking glass. Pour the sherry over top and add a pinch of flaky salt. Serve with a spoon and a platter of shortbread to be passed at the table.

Seeded Drop Biscuits

SERVES
6 to 8

TIME
30 minutes

INGREDIENTS
- 2 cups (250 g) all-purpose flour
- 1 tablespoon baking powder
- 1 tablespoon granulated sugar
- ½ teaspoon salt (omit if using salted butter)
- 6 tablespoons (85 g) cold butter, cut into small cubes
- 1 cup (240 ml) buttermilk, plus more as needed
- Seeds for topping, such as caraway seeds, poppy seeds, and toasted sesame seeds.
- Salted butter, honey, and jam (optional), for serving

The idea for these biscuits came from my late Nonni. We vacationed on Cape Cod when I was a child, and I have many memories of her baking them for us on misty, gray mornings. I remember the act of her making them was such a treat, and it clearly is where I get my love of *anything* seeded. Her original recipe calls for more sugar than I included here, and I've made a few other modifications, but the seeds remain! As I get older, I am less dogmatic about salted versus unsalted butter in recipes. I developed these using the former. If you use salted butter, omit the additional salt called for. These biscuits couldn't be easier to assemble, and they turn out light, flaky, and golden in about 30 minutes flat. They are great for breakfast with a mug of tea but would also pair nicely with a bowl of soup or stew. Alternatively, they can be used for dessert in something like a strawberry shortcake or even just a vanilla ice cream sandwich.

METHOD

Preheat the oven to 425°F (220°C). Line a large baking sheet with parchment paper.

In a large bowl, whisk together the flour, baking powder, sugar, and salt. Add the butter and with a pastry cutter or your hands, work the butter into the flour mixture to form coarse crumbs.

Stir in the buttermilk and mix gently until the dough just holds together and is slightly sticky. The dough should be relatively thick.

Using a medium-size ice cream scoop, scoop the dough onto the parchment-lined baking sheet, leaving about 1 inch (2.5 cm) or so between the biscuits. You should have 8 total.

Brush the top of each biscuit with a bit of buttermilk and top with a sprinkling of seeds of your choice.

Transfer to the oven and bake until golden, 12 to 14 minutes.

If desired, serve with salted butter, honey, and jam.

Rachel's Nutty Nuggets

MAKES
100 cookies

TIME
1½ hours

INGREDIENTS

1 pound (455 g/4 sticks) unsalted butter, at room temperature
1 cup (200 g) granulated sugar
1 large egg
4 teaspoons vanilla extract
4 cups (500 g) all-purpose flour
½ teaspoon kosher salt
1 bag (8 ounces/225 g) crushed pecans (about 2 cups)
1 bag (10 ounces/280 g) semisweet chocolate chips (about 2 cups)
1½ cups (150 g) powdered sugar, for dusting

This recipe yields a lot of cookies, approximately 100 nuggets! But, they are so addictively good, I'm hesitant to scale it down. They come courtesy of my friend, stylist Rachel Rumann, who makes them every year for Christmas. I had them and had to share them with you, too. The nuggets do not spread, allowing for up to 30 per baking sheet, so roughly an hour of baking time total. Not so bad! I recommend going for it and packaging some up for friends as gifts. You can also freeze them to pull out for coffee breaks.

METHOD

Preheat the oven to 350°F (180°C).

In a stand mixer fitted with the paddle (or in a large bowl using a hand mixer), beat the butter and granulated sugar on medium-high speed until the butter mixture is pale yellow, light, and fluffy, 7 to 10 minutes. Add the egg and vanilla and beat for a minute longer.

Reduce the mixer speed to low and gently and gradually beat in the flour and salt until incorporated.

Stir in the crushed pecans and chocolate chips until evenly combined with the dough.

Using a tablespoon to measure, shape the dough into balls and place them fairly close together (they don't spread) on a baking sheet.

Bake until the bottom of the cookie is golden, 15 to 18 minutes.

Transfer the cookies to a wire rack and let them cool for 15 to 20 minutes. In batches, drop into a brown paper bag with the powdered sugar and shake until coated.

Kate's Feast *of* Lost Days Shortbread *with* Star Anise and Orange

MAKES
1 (9-inch) shortbread

TIME
45 minutes

INGREDIENTS

- 3 whole star anise
- 8 ounces (225 g/2 sticks) chilled unsalted butter, cut into ½-inch (12 mm) pieces
- ½ cup (100 g) granulated sugar
- ¼ cup (25 g) powdered sugar
- ¾ teaspoon kosher salt
- 2½ cups (315 g) all-purpose flour
- Grated zest of 2 medium oranges (about 1 tablespoon)
- 1 large egg, beaten
- 2 tablespoons demerara sugar, for sprinkling

On a late August day, out of nowhere, my friend Kate Crasweller slid into my DMs with a note that read, "This is a last-minute invite, but I'm doing a beautiful dinner on an island tomorrow evening for friends. It's on the south shore, and I wonder if you want to come?All seasonal seafood and produce cooked outdoors and served at the table with our feet in the sand."

I've never said yes to an invitation so quickly. We also happened to be in a road trip frame of mind after a long weekend tooling around Cape Breton.

Kate shared one of the most special experiences I have ever could have dreamt up. Her friends were warm and welcoming. Christian free-dove deep for scallops, which we ate right out of their shells. Another friend brought oysters from his family's farm. Kate served cured salmon, steamed clams in broth with homemade sourdough, grilled chicken hearts, which she cooked over an open fire and served over polenta with chanterelles she had foraged and quick pickled. We ate on one long table on a bluff overlooking the Atlantic. We felt right at home and so welcomed among people we had just met. Sugo, our dog, had run of the entire island.

Kate called the dinner the inaugural Feast of Lost Days, as we had all lost so much time gathering over the pandemic. This was a way to reclaim that time together.

As it grew dark, lanterns were put out on the table and Kate passed this wonderful shortbread at the table for dessert. As we boarded the Boston Whaler back to the mainland, I kindly asked her if I could include it here on these pages. Luckily she said yes.

METHOD

Preheat the oven to 350°F (180°C).

In a small, dry skillet, toast the star anise over medium-high heat, tossing occasionally, until fragrant, about 2 minutes. Transfer to a mortar and pestle or mini food processor and grind until fine.

In a stand mixer fitted with the paddle (or in a large bowl using a hand mixer), cream the butter, granulated sugar, powdered sugar, and salt on medium-high speed until light and fluffy, 7 to 10 minutes. Reduce the speed to low and add the flour, ground star anise, and orange zest and mix until just combined.

Transfer the dough to a 9-inch (20 cm) round cake pan or springform pan and with your hands gently press in the dough. With a pastry brush, brush the dough with the beaten egg and sprinkle with the demerara sugar.

Bake until the shortbread is golden brown and the sides begin to pull away from the edges, 25 to 30 minutes.

Let cool in pan on a wire rack before turning out and cutting into wedges.

A Note: This is a very versatile and easy recipe to make. It's perfect for any celebration, including the holiday season—whether for a tree-trimming party or a family gathering. I love having some pre-made in the freezer year-round for impromptu guests. It pairs beautifully with a cup of tea.

CHAPTER 6 (224—241)

NICE TO KNOWS *AND* GOOD TO HAVES

Homemade Flatbread

MAKES
4 big or 6 small flatbreads

TIME
3½ hours (includes rising time)

INGREDIENTS

¾ cup (180 ml) warm water
1 (7 g) envelope instant yeast (2¼ teaspoons)
½ teaspoon granulated sugar
2½ cups (315 g) all-purpose flour
2 tablespoons extra-virgin olive oil
1 teaspoon kosher salt
¼ cup (60 ml) sour cream or whole-milk yogurt
Butter, for cooking

This recipe is adapted by Kelly Mariani, friend and chef at Scribe Winery. They are incredibly easy to pull together and worth the low-lift labor.

METHOD

In a bowl, whisk together the water, yeast, sugar, ½ cup (65 g) of the flour and let rest for 15 minutes. Add the remaining 2 cups (250 g) flour, the olive oil, salt, and sour cream.

Knead the dough for 2 minutes, then let it rest for 10 minutes covered with plastic. Knead it again for another minute and place into an oiled bowl. Cover the bowl with plastic and leave to rise on the counter for 2 hours.

Divide the dough into 4 or 6 equal portions, roll into balls, and dust with flour. Cover and leave to rise for 1 hour before baking.

Use your hands or a rolling pin to stretch or roll the dough out until it's about ¼ inch (6 mm) thick. Heat a pan over medium high heat, add a nub of butter, and cook the flatbreads on both sides until golden brown. (Alternatively, you can place the dough right onto an oiled grill.)

Smoky Tomato Butter

MAKES
about 2 cups (500 g)

TIME
20 minutes

INGREDIENTS

1 pint (300 g) cherry tomatoes
8 ounces (225 g) unsalted butter, at room temperature
½ teaspoon red pepper flakes
1 tablespoon 'nduja, at room temperature
Kosher salt

Stir into pasta, smear on toast, toss with roasted vegetables, or melt on top of fish or chicken.

METHOD

Preheat the broiler to high and place the tomatoes on a foil-lined baking sheet.

Broil the tomatoes until the skins blister and begin to brown, shaking the pan to brown all sides, 6 to 7 minutes.

Let the tomatoes cool to room temperature. This is very important, or it will melt the butter! I have lived this.

In a food processor, combine the tomatoes, butter, pepper flakes, and 'nduja and pulse until blended, but not completely smooth. Taste and season with salt as needed. Store in the fridge.

A Poached Chicken

MAKES
1 chicken, plus broth

TIME
1½ hours

INGREDIENTS

- 1 whole chicken (3 to 4 pounds/1.4 to 1.8 kg)
- 1 head garlic, halved horizontally
- 1 onion, halved
- 2 carrots, halved
- 2 celery stalks, halved
- 2 bay leaves
- 3 to 4 parsley sprigs
- A few thyme, rosemary, or sage sprigs (optional)
- 1 tablespoon peppercorns

Make this chicken and you'll have endless ways to use it for meals throughout the week. Soups, stews, pies, salads, and more. Plus, you now also have broth to sip, spoon into sauces, or use however you see fit.

METHOD

Place the chicken in a stockpot and add all the remaining ingredients. Cover with water, 5 to 6 quarts (4.7 to 5.7 L).

Cover and bring to a boil over high heat. Once boiling, reduce the heat to a simmer, partially cover, and cook for about 1½ hours.

Turn off the heat and remove the chicken. When it is cool enough to handle, take the meat off the bones.

Strain the broth and season it with salt. Eat or reserve the broth and meat for whatever you like.

Immersion Blender Aioli

MAKES
1 cup (240 ml)

TIME
5 minutes

INGREDIENTS

- 2 egg yolks
- 1 clove garlic, grated
- 2 teaspoons Dijon mustard
- 2 tablespoons fresh lemon juice
- ½ teaspoon kosher salt, plus more as needed
- ½ cup (120 ml) neutral oil, such as vegetable, canola, or grapeseed
- ½ cup (120 ml) extra-virgin olive oil

In my last book, I asked you to make aioli by whisking slowly and having patience. I am so sorry. I'm not doing that again, or likely ever. This method gets bright, garlicky, and perfect aioli on the table in moments, and I am thrilled about it; you will be, too. Not only do I like serving it with grilled squid, I love dolloping some on top of a frittata, swiping fried potatoes through it, and sometimes just sneaking a spoonful out of the fridge.

METHOD

Place the egg yolks, garlic, mustard, and lemon juice in the bottom of an immersion blender cup and then pour the oils over top. Place the immersion blender at the bottom of the cup and switch it on. Once you see it has begun to emulsify (this should happen almost immediately), slowly begin to lift the blender out of the cup, ensuring everything is indeed emulsified.

Transfer the mixture to a bowl, taste and adjust seasoning with more salt if needed. Store covered in the refrigerator for up to 1 week.

Mint *and* Caper Salsa Verde

MAKES
about 1 cup (240 ml)

TIME
10 minutes

INGREDIENTS

½ cup (25 g) finely chopped fresh Italian parsley

½ cup (25 g) finely chopped mint

2 tablespoons capers, rinsed well if in salt, and finely chopped

Grated zest of 1 lemon

2 tablespoons fresh lemon juice, plus more as needed

½ cup (120 ml) extra-virgin olive oil

Kosher salt

A green sauce is always good to have around to amp up weeknight dinners. Spoon it over meat, fish, chicken, or vegetables. It's also good stirred into yogurt for a quick dip.

METHOD

In a bowl, stir together the parsley, mint, capers, lemon zest, and lemon juice. Add the olive oil and stir together until well combined. Taste and adjust with salt and more lemon juice if needed.

Caramelized Onions

MAKES
about 1 cup (250 ml)

TIME
45 minutes

INGREDIENTS

- 2 tablespoons extra-virgin olive oil
- 2 tablespoons (30 g) unsalted butter
- 3 large yellow onions, halved and thinly sliced
- Kosher salt

Use these for pizza (page 150), toss them in pasta, make a caramelized onion dip, or put them on burgers. They do truly take 45 minutes to caramelize; anyone who tells you otherwise isn't telling the truth!

METHOD

In a large sauté pan, heat the olive oil and melt the butter over medium-low heat. Add the onions and season with salt. Cook, stirring the onions often, until they caramelize, about 45 minutes, adding in a few splashes of water to the pan if it starts to get dry in spots. Taste and adjust seasonings with salt to your liking.

The caramelized onions will keep for up to 1 week in the fridge and can be frozen for up to 6 months.

Broccoli Rabe *with* Toasted Garlic

SERVES
4

TIME
15 minutes

INGREDIENTS
Kosher salt
1 large bunch broccoli rabe, tough ends trimmed
3 tablespoons olive oil, plus more for serving
6 cloves garlic, smashed and peeled
½ teaspoon red pepper flakes
Freshly ground black pepper
Lemon half (optional), for serving

Use this method with any wiltable green: kale, escarole, mustard greens, baby bok choy—you name it. It's a quick and easy side.

METHOD

Bring a large pot of salted water to a boil. Add the broccoli rabe and blanch it for 2 to 3 minutes. Drain and set aside.

Meanwhile, in a 12-inch (30 cm) skillet, heat the olive oil over medium heat until it shimmers. Add the garlic and pepper flakes and cook, stirring frequently, until the garlic is golden brown and slightly crispy, 2 to 3 minutes.

Add the broccoli rabe to the skillet and toss it to coat in the garlic oil. Season with salt and pepper to your liking. Transfer to a platter and squeeze over some lemon juice, if desired.

Fried Shallots

MAKES
about 1 cup (250 ml)

TIME
15 minutes

INGREDIENTS

3 tablespoons neutral oil, such as canola or vegetable
3 large shallots, thinly sliced into rings
Flaky salt

Use these to put on top of salads, rice, pastas, soups, and stews for a nice, salty crunch. Like with all fried foods, you want to salt them as soon as they come out of the oil, so it adheres to the shallots.

METHOD

Line a plate with paper towels and have near the stove. In a 12-inch (30 cm) skillet, heat the oil over high heat until it shimmers. Add the shallots and cook, stirring occasionally, until crispy and golden, 3 to 5 minutes.

With a spider or slotted spoon, carefully transfer the shallots to the paper towels and sprinkle with flaky salt.

Shallots can be fried 3 days ahead. Store in an airtight container at room temperature.

Helen's Mustard Vinaigrette

MAKES
about 1 cup (250 ml)

TIME
10 minutes

INGREDIENTS

1 shallot, finely chopped
2 tablespoons good-quality white or red wine vinegar or lemon juice
Kosher salt
1 teaspoon Dijon mustard
½ teaspoon honey
¾ cup (180 ml) olive oil
1 teaspoon finely chopped fresh herbs (optional), such as thyme, Italian parsley, or whatever is in season
Freshly ground black pepper

My dearest Helen is a very good cook, but often gets relegated to salad dressing maker, because Dan and I have a tendency to dominate in the kitchen, and the dressing is very good. I always ask her to make it, and this is a riff on her classic.

METHOD

In a medium bowl, stir together the shallot and vinegar with a pinch of salt and let sit for 5 minutes or so. Whisk in the mustard and honey.

Slowly drizzle in the oil, whisking until the mixture is emulsified. Stir in the herbs (if using). Season to taste with more salt as needed and pepper.

A Note: I often have the end of a Maille mustard jar going in the fridge. If you do, too, you could add all the ingredients (sans mustard) to the mustard jar, seal the lid tightly, and give it a good shake until everything is emulsified. Season to taste with more salt as needed and pepper.

New Potatoes *and* Mint *with* Too Much Butter

SERVES
4

TIME
20 minutes

INGREDIENTS

- 2 pounds (910 g) small new potatoes or baby Yukon Gold potatoes
- ⅓ cup (45 g) kosher salt, plus more to taste
- 1 large bunch of mint, 2 tablespoons finely chopped and reserved
- 8 tablespoons (115 g/1 stick) unsalted butter, cut into pieces
- Freshly ground black pepper
- Flaky salt, for finishing

My favorite Brit, Helen, told me that her nan boiled potatoes with a fistful of mint in the water to subtly flavor it and I loved it so much, I've included it here. I toss the potatoes in an absurd amount of butter and top them with fresh mint, because we love mint in this house. Parsley or chives as a topping is always lovely.

METHOD

Place the potatoes in a large pot and cover them with water. Add the kosher salt and a fistful of mint and bring to a boil.

Reduce the heat and simmer until the potatoes are tender, about 10 minutes. You can pierce them with a fork to make sure. The time will depend on the size of your potatoes, so check frequently.

Drain the potatoes and discard the mint. Return the potatoes to the pot and set it over low heat. Add the butter and toss until the potatoes are fully coated in the melted butter. Taste and adjust seasoning with more salt if needed and black pepper.

Transfer to a bowl and top with 2 tablespoons finely chopped mint and a few pinches of flaky salt.

Creamy Polenta

SERVES
4

TIME
10 minutes

INGREDIENTS

4 cups (1 L) water or chicken stock
1 teaspoon kosher salt, plus more to taste
1 cup (180 g) polenta
3 tablespoons (45 g) unsalted butter
⅓ cup (75 g) mascarpone
Freshly ground black pepper

This makes a perfect side to braised meats and vegetables. I add butter and mascarpone cheese to really make it rich and over the top. Alternatively, you could use crème fraîche or even stir in some heavy cream. It's incredibly comforting.

METHOD

In a saucepan, bring the water or stock and salt to a boil. Slowly whisk in the polenta. Reduce the heat to a simmer and continue to whisk the polenta until there are no clumps. Continue stirring frequently until the polenta is soft, tender, and thickened, 4 to 6 minutes.

Remove from the heat and stir in the butter and the mascarpone. Taste and adjust seasonings with more salt as needed and black pepper.

Chicory *and* Fennel Salad

SERVES
4 to 6

TIME
10 minutes

INGREDIENTS

- 2 medium heads radicchio, leaves separated and torn, or 1 large head escarole
- 1 medium fennel bulb, halved, cored, and thinly sliced (I like to use a mandoline)
- 1 cup (130 g) toasted nuts, such as pistachios or walnuts, roughly chopped
- Kosher salt and freshly ground black pepper
- Helen's Mustard Vinaigrette (page 234) or lemon juice and olive oil, for serving

This is probably the salad I make the most. I always have radicchio or another bitter green in my fridge and you should, too. A thinly sliced blood or navel orange would be a lovely addition to this as would some Castelvetrano olives and a few tablespoons of roughly chopped chives or mint, or both.

METHOD

In a large bowl, combine the radicchio, fennel, and half the nuts. Season with salt and pepper.

Add some of the vinaigrette and toss until the leaves are coated. Taste and adjust seasonings as needed with salt and pepper. Top with the remaining nuts.

A Bacon Sarnie

SERVES
1

TIME
10 minutes

INGREDIENTS

2 to 3 rashers smoked back bacon
2 slices white sandwich bread (I like Pepperidge Farm)
Unsalted butter, at room temperature
HP sauce

A choose-your-own-adventure British breakfast staple. Best served on Boxing Day morning or another morning when you need a little bit of TLC.

METHOD

Cook the bacon however you'd prefer, on the stove or in the oven.

Meanwhile, toast the bread. Butter one side of each piece of bread, liberally!

Place the bacon on one of the pieces of bread. On the other, add as much HP sauce as you like. Smash together and cut on the diagonal and have a big mug of PG Tips at the ready.

A Note: For those not from across the pond, HP is a British brown sauce. Its main ingredients are tomatoes, malt, vinegar, and molasses. The only thing I can think to compare it to is steak sauce, which I am not fond of, but for some reason I adore HP sauce. You can find it in most American grocery stores nowadays.

Roasted tomatoes for Butter Rice with Roasted Tomatoes and Herbs **(58)**

Menus
to Consider

A HOLIDAY DINNER

Fried Sausage–Stuffed Olives with Sesame **(24)**
A Christmas Lasagna **(126)**
Chicory and Fennel Salad **(237)**
Brandy Alexanders **(214)**

A FEAST *of* SOME FISHES

Scallop Crudo with Blood Orange and Mint **(28)**
Italian Shrimp Toast **(22)**
Spicy Crab Pasta with Toasted Lemon Crumbs **(118)**
Rachel's Nutty Nougats **(220)**
Rosato or other medium-bodied rosé

A CELEBRATION COCKTAIL PARTY

Crab Mayonnaise-y with Toast **(26)**
Smashed Potatoes with Sour Cream and Caviar **(32)**
Spicy and Jammy Agrodolce Peppers with Fried Salumi **(20)**
Very good cheese and charcuterie
Bubbles

A DINNER PARTY

Lamb Chops with a Salad of Dates, Toasted Garlic, Walnuts, and Parsley **(184)**
Butter Rice with Roasted Tomatoes and Herbs **(58)**
Roasted Carrots with Cilantro Yogurt and Roasted Pistachios **(72)**
Dark chocolate and citrus
Pinot Noir

A LATE LUNCH AFTER A BRISK WINTER WALK

Golden and Crispy Leeks with Melted Gruyère **(56)**
An Excellent Lentil Stew with Pork, Crispy Walnuts, and Lemon **(92)**
Arugula salad tossed with Helen's Mustard Vinaigrette **(234)**
Kate's Feast of Lost Days Shortbread with Star Anise and Orange **(222)**

A SUNDAY SUPPER

Fennel Gratin with Olives and Provolone **(88)**
Calabrian Chili and Pickled Pepper–Braised Pork in Tomato **(202)**
Creamy Polenta **(236)**
Broccoli Rabe with Toasted Garlic **(232)**
Bakery-bought rainbow cookies or cannolis
The Ventura: an Amaro Spritz **(34)**

A SPRING GARDEN LUNCH

Spicy Shrimp Butter **(36)** with toast
Peas, Shoots, and Leaves with Buttermilk and Feta Dressing **(68)**
Shaved Asparagus Salad with Comté, Toasted Almonds, and Fried Prosciutto **(64)**
Seeded Drop Biscuits **(218)** with strawberries and whipped cream

A SUMMER MAGIC HOUR

A Lobster Dip Welcome **(42)**
Snacking Peppers **(52)**
Hélène's Roasted Olive Dip with Za'atar and Sumac **(38)**
The Conversation Starter **(48)**

A BEACH PICNIC

A Perfect Beach Sandwich **(46)**
Roasted Eggplant Dip with Toasted Seeds **(50)**
Smoky Toasted Corn Salad with Fried Shallots **(82)**
Potato chips
Cold beer

A SIMPLE SUMMER DINNER

Oysters and grilled sausages
Tomato Salad with Anchovy Bread Crumbs **(74)**
Snappy and Herby Potato Salad with Frizzled Leeks **(86)**
Rye Blueberry Galette **(210)**
Rosé

A FEW EASY WEEKNIGHT DINNERS

Fluke with Panko Walnut Crumbs and Broccolini **(166)**
Harissa and Brown Sugar Glazed Salmon **(178)**
Simplest Potato and Leek Soup with Blue Cheese Toasts **(94)**
Chickpea Fennel Stew with Swiss Chard and Fried Lemon **(102)**
Roast Chicken with Lemon, Fennel, and Crispy Pecorino Potatoes **(182)**

Acknowledgments

Cookbooks touch so many hands (and mouths!) before they make their way to yours. It is no small feat to create these jewellike capsules of time and place, and I feel incredibly lucky to do this work.

None of it would be possible without my lovely, ever-upbeat (no matter the struggle) editor, Holly Dolce. We got there in the end, didn't we? Creative Director Diane Shaw, thank you for your keen eye and endless patience. And Natasha Martin, can you believe we're still doing this together? I appreciate you more than you know. To Hannah Braden and the entire team at Abrams, thank you.

To my wildly talented designer, Sebit Min, your enthusiasm and creativity were evident from the start. You are a true delight, and the design world is lucky to have you in it.

Pearl Jones, there is no better food stylist. I'm grateful to you for so many things. You too, Kayla Wong! Thank you for everything. Rebecca Bartoshesky, you're the cream of the crop in all you do—in this case, props. (And I'm sorry I never finished *ACOTAR*.) Dimity Jones, you too are a gift—just look at the fennel gratin! All of you made this book look exquisite.

To Kate Crasweller, Sarah Copeland, Sarah Raimo, Alexis deBoschnek, Deanne Fitzpatrick and Robert Mansour, Paula and Phil Forman, Harry Guinness and Sophie von Haselberg, Emma and Dom Harding, Hélène and John Heath, Suzy Pasette, Annabel Taylor and John Panzer, Kevin Tienharra and Tom Champine, Ali Stafford, Hannah Sullivan, and Steph Whitaker: Thank you for eating, drinking, recipe testing, cheering, and inspiring me.

Rachel Rumman, thank you for styling me, testing recipes, holding a bounce, jumping in wherever needed, and for your own recipe too. Andy Wilhelm, I'm looking at you as well. We're so grateful to have you celebrity hobos in our lives.

Chad Silver and Martin Seck, *meine Lieben*, you two photographed this beautiful book, and I am forever grateful for your time, energy, and devotion to finding the perfect light. You should really work together more often.

To my chosen family, Helen Dealtry, Dan Barry, and Kelly Marages, how did I ever get so lucky? Some things are meant to be.

And to my Chad, I love you so much, you're thanked twice. Thank you for your support, your patience, your attention to detail, and our life together. You said we could do it—we did.

Index

Editor:
Holly Dolce

Designer:
Sebit Min

Design Manager:
Danielle Youngsmith

Managing Editor:
Amy Vinchesi

Production Manager:
Kathleen Gaffney

Library of Congress Control Number: 2025938002

ISBN: 978-1-4197-4970-4
eISBN: 979-8-89684-250-7

Printed and bound in China
10 9 8 7 6 5 4 3 2 1

Abrams books are available at special discounts when purchased in quantity for premiums and promotions as well as fundraising or educational use. Special editions can also be created to specification. For details, contact specialsales@abramsbooks.com or the address below.

ABRAMS is represented in the UK and Europe by Abrams & Chronicle Books, 1 West Smithfield, London EC1A 9JU and Média-Participations, 57 rue Gaston Tessier, 75166 Paris, France.
abramsandchronicle.co.uk and media-participations.com
info@abramsandchronicle.co.uk